Praise for *25 Need-to-Know MBA Models*

'Whether you are a potential business school student or an experienced executive, this is the must-have reference guide to MBA models. I wish this book had been around when I did my MBA! At last, the definitive reference guide to MBA models packed full of useful tips and practical suggestions.'

Stephen Martin, Director General, Institute of Directors

'This book is an essential tool for anyone working in management today. It explains in clear terms the important management models and techniques that are widely used, and what management need to do next if they want to learn more.'

Shinsuke Toda, Managing Director, Head of Europe Department, Mizuho Bank

'Captures brilliantly the key ways businesses think and act in an easy-to-read book. Complex business frameworks made easy to understand, with helpful tips and guidance.'

Dr Matt Carter, Founder, Message House

25 need-to-know MBA models

Pearson

At Pearson, we believe in learning – all kinds of learning for all kinds of people. Whether it's at home, in the classroom or in the workplace, learning is the key to improving our life chances.

That's why we're working with leading authors to bring you the latest thinking and best practices, so you can get better at the things that are important to you. You can learn on the page or on the move, and with content that's always crafted to help you understand quickly and apply what you've learned.

If you want to upgrade your personal skills or accelerate your career, become a more effective leader or more powerful communicator, discover new opportunities or simply find more inspiration, we can help you make progress in your work and life.

Every day our work helps learning flourish, and wherever learning flourishes, so do people.

To learn more, please visit us at **www.pearson.com/uk**

The Financial Times

With a worldwide network of highly respected journalists, *The Financial Times* provides global business news, insightful opinion and expert analysis of business, finance and politics. With over 500 journalists reporting from 50 countries worldwide, our in-depth coverage of international news is objectively reported and analysed from an independent, global perspective.

To find out more, visit **www.ft.com**

25 need-to-know MBA models

Julian Birkinshaw and Ken Mark

 Pearson

Harlow, England • London • New York • Boston • San Francisco • Toronto • Sydney
Dubai • Singapore • Hong Kong • Tokyo • Seoul • Taipei • New Delhi
Cape Town • São Paulo • Mexico City • Madrid • Amsterdam • Munich • Paris • Milan

Pearson Education Limited
Edinburgh Gate
Harlow CM20 2JE
United Kingdom
Tel: +44 (0)1279 623623
Web: www.pearson.com/uk

First edition published 2017 (print and electronic)

The rights of Julian Birkinshaw and Ken Mark to be identified as authors of this work have been asserted by them in accordance with the Copyright, Designs and Patents Act 1988.

ISBN: 978-1-292-17889-9 (print)
        978-1-292-17890-5 (PDF)
        978-1-292-17891-2 (ePub)

British Library Cataloguing-in-Publication Data
A catalogue record for the print edition is available from the British Library

Library of Congress Cataloging-in-Publication Data
A catalog record for the print edition is available from the Library of Congress

10 9 8 7 6 5 4 3 2 1
21 20 19 18 17

Cover design by Two Associates
Print edition typeset in 9 Stone Serif ITC Pro by SPi Global
Printed and bound in Great Britain by Ashford Colour Press Ltd, Gosport, Hampshire

NOTE THAT ANY PAGE CROSS REFERENCES REFER TO THE PRINT EDITION

Contents

About the authors

Julian Birkinshaw is Professor of Strategy and Entrepreneurship at the London Business School and Director of the Deloitte Institute of Innovation and Entrepreneurship. He is the author of 13 books, including *Fast/Forward*, *Reinventing Management* and *Becoming a Better Boss*.

Ken Mark is CEO of The Martello Group. He was Finance Director at Diversified Resources International and worked for Procter & Gamble and Harvard Business School. He has written case studies for Harvard, Ivey Business School and the London Business School.

Acknowledgements

We would like to thank our colleagues at London Business School, Ivey School of Business and other schools for their advice on selecting the management models. In particular, we thank Dr Colette Southam of Bond University, Australia, for reviewing several sections of the book. We also thank our students, in particular those in the EMBA and MBA programmes at London Business School, for providing input into our selection process.

Publisher's acknowledgements

We are grateful to the following for permission to reproduce copyright material:

Figure on p 65 adapted from The BCG Portfolio Matrix from the Product Portfolio Matrix, © 1970, The Boston Consulting Group (BCG); figure on p 84 adapted from Porter, M.E. (1979) 'How competitive forces shape strategy', *Harvard Business Review*, March/April: 21–38. Copyright © 1979 by the Harvard Business School Publishing Corporation, all rights reserved. Reprinted by permission of Harvard Business Review; figure on p 106 adapted from Christensen, C.M. (1997) *The Innovator's Dilemma: When new technologies cause great firms to fail.* Boston, MA: Harvard Business Review Press. Copyright © 1997 by the Harvard Business School Publishing Corporation, all rights reserved. Reprinted by permission of Harvard Business Review.

Introduction

There are many models and frameworks in use in the business world today, and it is hard to keep track of them all. We wrote this book to help you make sense of the most important of these models – to understand where they came from, when you might use them, how to use them and what are their biggest benefits and weaknesses.

The title *25 need-to-know MBA models* reflects the fact that these models are all taught to students at business schools seeking to get an MBA (Masters in Business Administration). The MBA is a generalist degree – in other words, it is designed to provide students with a broad grounding in all the key aspects of business. This book reflects the breadth of the MBA. It has five sections, each one corresponding to a typical core course in the first year of an MBA programme. While we only discuss five models in each section, we also make reference to other important models, to give you a flavour of the scope of the materials covered in such a core course.

Who should read this book? If you are doing an MBA, this is an easy-to-access summary of the key models you are being taught, with useful pointers about how they should be applied, and follow-up readings if you want to know more.

If you are an executive or a manager who didn't go to business school, the book is a valuable reference guide. If your subordinates or colleagues start throwing out unfamiliar terms they picked up at a business school, you will want to know what they are talking about. Most of the concepts in the world of business are actually pretty straightforward – this book provides enough details on twenty-five of the most important ones to get you up to speed.

Finally, the book should also be of interest to prospective MBA students, who are studying in advance of entering an MBA programme or who are fascinated by the prospect of doing an MBA. If the models and concepts described here look valuable and interesting, then you should take the plunge and sign up for a programme. While we have covered the 'need-to-know' models here, it goes without saying that you learn vastly more in the course of an MBA programme than could ever be picked up in a single text.

What is included?

In researching this book, we reviewed the course materials at the business schools we work with, or where we have good friends (e.g. London Business School, Richard Ivey School of Business INSEAD, Wharton, Harvard), and we sought to identify the most important models, frameworks and concepts that students were taught during their 'core' courses. (In most programmes, the core courses are followed by a range of 'elective' courses that allow students to specialise.) We also market-tested our initial selection with a group of students and graduates, by asking them how important they thought each model was. This allowed us to fine-tune our choices.

While our selection process was careful, the final list of models is still highly subjective. It is a bit like choosing the most influential people in history, or the best movies of the last twenty years: there is some data you can use to support your choices, but ultimately there is a lot of judgment involved, and we wouldn't expect anyone else to agree 100 per cent with the list we finally settled on. One important criterion we used, for example, was deliberately to include a mix of 'classic' and 'contemporary' models in each section, so you can develop some perspective on the evolution of the subject matter.

The book is organised into five parts, corresponding to five of the most important areas or topics that are taught in an MBA programme. Each section includes the five 'need-to-know' models, arranged in alphabetical order, and at the beginning of each section we have written a brief overview to explain how the models we chose fit together. Of course, there are many important topics in each of these areas that we don't have space to cover. The further readings listed at the end of each chapter provide useful pointers for where to get additional information.

We will be the first to acknowledge that our chosen structure is a very traditional way of looking at the business world. Some business schools have sought to develop cross-disciplinary or integrative approaches to their teaching, for example by focusing on real-world business challenges. But they are in the minority – the vast majority of business schools still organise their courses as we have done here.

To keep the book to a reasonable length, we have had to make some tough choices. We have not included any models that describe the 'macro' business environment, whether in terms of economic theory, government policy, law, or trade regulations. We have steered clear of basic statistical models and tools, and we have spent relatively little time on individual-level psychological issues, or on the challenges of starting a business from scratch. We also made the tricky decision not to have sections on accounting or operations management. These are important topics, but in our experience they are becoming less central to the curriculum in business schools, and decreasing numbers of MBA students are moving into jobs in these areas. As a general rule, we have focused on issues that are the concern of the firm or business as a whole. Ultimately, these are things that a 'general manager' in a firm needs to know.

What is a 'model'?

We have used the term 'model' very loosely in this book to include frameworks, concepts, models and tools. We decided that it was more important to cover the key ideas that MBA students are exposed to in their core courses, than to stick narrowly to a diction-ary definition. For example, 'open innovation' is an important concept in the world of innovation and strategy today, so we have a chapter on it, even though it isn't a model as such.

Technically speaking, a *model* is a simplified version of something more complex – it helps you understand a specific phenomenon by identifying its key elements. A *framework* is a way of structuring your understanding of a multi-faceted phenomenon, often by pulling together a number of diverse elements. A *concept* is a high-level idea, a way of looking at the world that provides new insight. And a *tool* is a practical way of applying a body of thinking to address a particular task. These distinctions are of academic interest only; what matters is that this book includes what we believe to be the most important models, frameworks, concepts and tools in each area.

How you should read this book

For most readers, this is primarily a reference book – something to dip into, to remind you what a particular model is for, or to help you understand a concept you haven't heard of before. For others, it might be a way to get up to speed on an entire subject. If you are moving into a marketing role, for example, it would be very useful to read up on the five marketing models included here to make sure you understand the lie of the land. There may also be readers who are entering the business world for the first time, in which case reading the whole book from start to finish would make sense.

Julian Birkinshaw
Ken Mark

part
one

Management

Management is the art of getting work done through others. It involves marshalling a set of resources to achieve desired objectives. This section of the book provides a selection of important models and perspectives to help individuals do their jobs as managers more effectively.

What are the key things managers do? First, they make decisions about allocating people and money in an effective way. There are many analytical tools to help decision making, including decision trees and net present value analysis, but our focus here is on the behavioural side of things. Most decision making is not as rational as we might expect it to be. The chapter on **cognitive biases in decision making** discusses why people often make snap judgements that are flawed, and how effective managers can overcome these biases to make better decisions. There is also a chapter on **negotiating techniques,** with a specific focus on **BATNA** (best alternative to a negotiated agreement) that describes tactics for making decisions while in negotiation with others.

Second, a large part of effective management is about motivating others to take on work and do it in an effective way. This is hard because every individual has their own unique set of personal drivers, so that what works for one person may not work for the next. There is a chapter on **emotional intelligence** to tackle this question of how we understand and relate to others.

Finally, management involves making change happen. In large organisations there are standard, routine ways of working that everyone is comfortable with, so keeping things moving in an existing direction is actually very straightforward. But shifting the focus in another direction is where management gets difficult. John **Kotter's eight-step change management model** is described as a well-known way of approaching this difficult challenge.

We often make a distinction between management and leadership, where management is about getting work done through others, and leadership is a process of social influence. Every executive really needs to be good at both, as they are complementary activities. But being an effective leader is difficult because, ultimately, it is about how others perceive you. To be a good leader, you therefore need to know yourself as well as you know your people. This is partly about emotional intelligence, as described earlier. It is also about getting feedback from others. So, the final model in this section is **360-degree assessment,** which is a tool that leaders increasingly use to understand their own strengths and weaknesses.

Change management: Kotter's eight-step model

Many executives struggle to implement change in their organisations, and the larger the firm, the bigger the challenge. There are many recipe books for how to implement a change programme, and John Kotter's eight-step model is probably the most well-regarded.

When to use it

- To implement a change in your organisation – for example, a new formal structure, a new IT system or a different way of serving your customers.
- To diagnose why an earlier attempt at making a change has failed, and to come up with a corrective course of action.

Origins

The challenge of managing change has existed for as long as organisations have existed. However, it was only when researchers started to understand the behavioural aspects of organisations, and the notion that employees might resist a change they didn't buy into, that our modern view of change management started to emerge. For example, Kurt Lewin, an academic at MIT in the 1940s, showed how it was important to get employees out of their existing way of looking at the world before attempting a major change.

Systematic approaches to change management started to emerge in the post-war years, often led by consulting companies such as McKinsey and The Boston Consulting Group (BCG). During the 1980s and 1990s there were several attempts made to formalise and codify the process. The eight-step model proposed by Harvard professor John Kotter is probably the most well-known. Others include Claes Janssen's 'four rooms of change' model and Rosabeth Moss Kanter's 'change wheel'.

What it is

Change management is difficult partly because it appears easy. However, inertia is a very powerful force and we are all innately suspicious of attempts to disrupt the status quo in our organisations. Executives responsible for setting the strategy of the organisation will often see threats and opportunities much more clearly than those in more narrow roles, so a large part of their job in any change is about communicating why change is necessary. John Kotter's eight-step model therefore is all about 'people' – it is about how you get employees to adopt a planned change, making the required changes in their work patterns and attitudes. Kotter's model has eight steps, which should be undertaken in the prescribed order:

1 Create urgency

2 Form a powerful coalition

3 Create a vision for change

4 Communicate the vision

5 Remove obstacles

6 Create short-term wins

7 Build on the change

8 Anchor the changes in corporate culture.

How to use it

Kotter provides a great deal of detail about how each step of the model should be implemented. Obviously, much depends on the specific circumstances, and a leader should always be prepared to adapt the change plan depending on the reaction he or she receives. Below is a brief description of how to do each step.

Step 1: create urgency

This is about convincing employees in the organisation that there are problems or opportunities that need addressing. For example, Stephen Elop, the CEO of Nokia in 2012, tried to create urgency for change by talking about the 'burning platform' that Nokia was on – and how they needed to be prepared to consider dramatic changes to their business model.

Urgency can also be created by starting an honest dialogue with employees about what's happening in the market-place. Often, customer-facing staff can be your strongest allies in this regard as they have daily direct feedback about the market. If many people start talking about the need for change, the urgency can build and feed on itself.

Step 2: form a powerful coalition

While you, as the leader, need to take charge of a major change effort, you cannot do it on your own. So it is important to get key opinion leaders from within the organisation to work with you. You can find effective opinion leaders throughout the organisation – they don't necessarily follow the traditional company hierarchy. These people need to commit visibly to the change, and then to champion the change within their own part of the organisation.

Step 3: create a vision for change

Often people have very different views of what the future might look like. As leader, you need to create and articulate a clear vision so that people can see what it means to them – how it taps into their own interests, and how they might be able to contribute. You don't have to do this alone – involving key staff at this stage speeds up implementation later on as they feel more ownership for the change and have a bigger stake in its success.

Step 4: communicate the vision

In large organisations it is very difficult to get your message across to everyone, as there are often many layers between you (as a leader) and those operating on the front line. Effective leaders spend a lot of time giving talks, addressing people through multiple media and using their own direct subordinates to help spread the word.

Step 5: remove obstacles

Even a well-articulated and communicated vision doesn't get everyone on board. There will always be some people resisting, or some structures that get in the way. So you need to work actively to remove obstacles and empower the people you need to execute the vision.

Step 6: create short-term wins

People have short attention spans, so you need to provide some tangible evidence that things are moving in the right direction early on – typically within a few months. Of course, there is often some 'game playing' here, in that the quick wins are often under-way before the change programme has started. But that rarely detracts from the value they provide in creating momentum.

Step 7: build on the change

Kotter argues that many change projects fail because victory is declared too early. Quick wins are important, but you need to keep on looking for improvements, so that the organisation doesn't slide back into its old ways of working.

Step 8: anchor the changes in corporate culture

Finally, to make any change stick it needs to become part of the everyday way of working. This means embedding it in your corporate culture – telling stories about the change process and what made it successful, recognising key members of the original change coalition and including the change ideals and values when hiring and training new staff.

Top practical tip

Change management is all about people, and about making relatively small shifts in the way they behave. According to Kotter, your role as a leader is therefore about engaging with employees at an emotional level. They have to be able to 'see' the change (for example, through eye-catching situations where problems are resolved) and to 'feel' it (such as by gaining some sort of emotional response that motivates them to act). This helps to reinforce the desired behaviours.

Top pitfall

The Kotter model is very good for top-down change, where the top executives are motivated to change and have a well-informed view of where the organisation needs to go. There are some organisations, unfortunately, where these assumptions do not hold, in which case Kotter's model does not work. Such organisations either need a change in leadership, or they need a bottom-up process of change.

Further reading

For information on the 'four rooms of change' go to
www.claesjanssen.com

Kanter, R.M. (1992) *The Challenge of Organizational Change: How companies experience it and leaders guide it.* New York: Free Press.

Kotter, J. (1996) *Leading Change.* Boston, MA: Harvard Business School Press.

2

Cognitive biases in decision making

A cognitive bias is a way of interpreting and acting on information that is not strictly rational. For example, you might hire a candidate for a job because they went to the same school as you. There are many types of cognitive bias – with both positive and negative consequences – so it is important to understand how they work.

When to use it

- To understand how you make decisions, so that you can avoid making bad ones.
- To understand how others reach their point of view in discussions.
- To influence the decision-making processes in your organisation.

Origins

While there is a long history of research on cognitive biases, most people agree that the 'fathers' of the field are psychologists Amos Tversky and Daniel Kahneman. During the 1960s they conducted research seeking to understand why people often made flawed decisions. At that point in time, most people believed in 'rational choice theory', which suggested that humans would make logical and rational deductions based on the evidence available. However, Tversky and Kahneman showed conclusively that this is not so. For example, when faced with the prospect of losing £1,000, individuals become very risk-averse; whereas the prospect of winning the same amount of money encourages them to become risk-takers. This insight, among many others, helped them to develop an entirely new way of looking at decision making. Humans don't use algorithms, in the way a computer might. Rather, they use *heuristics*, or rules of thumb, that are simple to compute but introduce systematic errors.

Kahneman and Tversky's experiments spawned an entire stream of research that spread beyond psychology into other disciplines, including medicine and political science. More recently, the field of economics embraced their ideas, resulting in the creation of behavioural economics and the awarding of the Nobel Prize in Economics to Kahneman in 2002.

What it is

Cognitive bias is a general term used to describe the workings of the human mind that may lead to perceptual distortion, inaccurate judgement or illogical interpretation.

Cognitive biases come in many different forms. Some affect decision making – for example, the well-known tendency for groups to default into consensus ('groupthink') or to fail to see the truth in assembled data ('representativeness'). Some affect individual judgement – for example, making something appear more likely because of what it is associated with ('illusory correlation'), while others affect the workings of our memory – for example, by making past attitudes similar to present ones ('consistency bias'). There are also biases that affect individual motivation, such as the desire for a positive self-image ('egocentric bias'). The table below lists some of the most well-known examples of cognitive bias.

How to use it

The main way you use cognitive biases in the workplace is by being aware of their existence, and then taking steps to avoid their damaging side effects. For example, imagine you are in a business meeting and you are being asked to decide whether to go ahead with a proposal to launch a new product. Because of your knowledge of cognitive biases, you ask yourself a number of questions:

- Is there a reason to think that the people making the recommendation are suffering from bias, for example confirmation bias in their assessment of the potential market size, or are they trying to manipulate the group into a decision based on how they have framed the problem?
- Was there a high-quality discussion around the table? Did people have an opportunity to voice their concerns? Was the relevant information brought to bear on the discussion? Or did minority voices get drowned out?

On the basis of this analysis, it is your job to counter the biases that you think may be creeping in. For example, if you think someone is being selective with the data they are presenting, you can ask an independent expert to provide their own set of data. If you think a meeting has reached agreement too soon, you can call on someone to put forward a counter-argument. One of the most important jobs of the chairman in a meeting, in fact, is to be conscious of these potential biases and to use his or her experience to avoid egregious errors.

Much the same logic applies to other aspects of work in organisations. When discussing the performance of a subordinate, or when talking to a potential customer, you need always to be alert to the likely cognitive biases they have, and how these might get in the way of a good outcome. There are so many cognitive biases out there that it takes many years of experience to master this process.

Examples of cognitive biases

Name	Description
Framing	The relative appeal or value of an option or an item fluctuates depending on how it is presented. For example, we expect to pay more for a Coke in a 5* hotel than at a railway station vending machine. Context is key.
Confirmation bias	The tendency to search for information in a way that confirms our preconceptions and discredits information that does not support our view.
Fundamental attribution error	The tendency for us to overemphasise personality-based explanations for behaviours observed in others. If a driver in front of us swerves unexpectedly, our automatic reaction is to label him a 'bad driver', whereas in fact he might have swerved to avoid something lying on the road.
Availability	The more easily we can recall an event or a group of people, the more common we perceive these events or people to be.
Representativeness	When we are asked to judge the probability that an object belongs to a particular category, our estimate is based on how representative that object is of the category, and it ignores the underlying distribution.
Anchoring	Establishing the perceived value of something at an arbitrarily high or low level. This is commonly observed in negotiations, for example with a salesperson setting a high price and then discounting it, making us feel as though we have got a better deal.

Top practical tip

Here is a specific tip for managing a meeting, put forward by Daniel Kahneman. Before a difficult decision has to be made, ask everyone around the table to write down their views on a piece of paper. Then, when it is their turn to speak, they have to say what they wrote on their paper. This avoids people being swayed in their opinions by what the person before them said.

Top pitfalls

It is possible to abuse your knowledge of cognitive biases by over-analysing things. In many business contexts, speed of decision making is important, so all the techniques described above are helpful but they can also slow things down a lot. The trick, as always, is about balance – the right blend of careful analytical thinking and intuition-based judgement.

The other big pitfall is that it is much easier to recognise cognitive biases in others than in yourself, so don't make the mistake of thinking you are immune from bias. Ask others to guide you on this – task them to challenge your thinking, and to tell you if you are falling into one of the traps we have discussed above.

Further reading

Kahneman, D. (2012) *Thinking, Fast and Slow.* London: Penguin Books.

Rosenzweig, P. (2007) *The Halo Effect.* New York: Free Press.

Thaler, R.H. and Sunstein, C.R. (2008) *Nudge: Improving decisions about health, wealth, and happiness.* New Haven, CT: Yale University Press.

3

Emotional intelligence

Emotional intelligence is the ability to monitor your own and other people's emotions. This helps you to discriminate between different emotions and label them appropriately, which in turn helps you to guide your thinking and behaviour and increase your personal effectiveness.

When to use it

- To help you do your job as a manager or a leader of others.
- To decide who to hire or promote.
- To assess and improve the quality of leadership across an organisation.

Origins

The concept of emotional intelligence has been around for many decades. Its origins lie with research done by Edward Thorndike in the 1930s, who came up with the notion of 'social intelligence', or the ability to get along with others. In the 1970s Howard Gardner, the educational psychologist, showed that there were multiple forms of intelligence, which helped to legitimise the idea that less academically trained forms of intelligence were important. The term 'emotional intelligence' was first used by researcher Wayne Payne in 1985, in his doctoral dissertation.

Since then, three different approaches to emotional intelligence have emerged. The *ability model* of Peter Salovey and John Mayer focuses on the individual's ability to process emotional information and use it to navigate the social environment. The *trait model* of K.V. Petrides focuses on an individual's self-perceived attributes – it sees emotional intelligence as a set of human traits. The third and most popular approach, put forward by author Daniel Goleman, is a blend of the other two, in that it combines abilities and traits.

What it is

There are many different types of human intelligence – some people are good at mathematics, some are good with words, others have musical skills or good hand–eye coordination. Emotional intelligence is one such type of intelligence. It is very hard to measure, but it turns out to be vitally important in the workplace, and especially for leaders of organisations. One of the hallmarks of great leaders, it is argued, is that they are good at sensing how others are feeling, and adapting their message and their style of interaction accordingly. Great leaders are also very aware of their own strengths and weaknesses, which is another important facet of emotional intelligence.

The popular model of emotional intelligence put forward by Daniel Goleman concentrates on five components:

1 **Self-awareness:** the ability to recognise and understand personal moods and emotions and drives, and their effect on others.
2 **Self-regulation:** the ability to control disruptive impulses and moods, suspend judgement and think before acting.
3 **Internal motivation:** a passion to work for internal reasons that go beyond money and status.

4 **Empathy:** the ability to understand the emotional make-up of other people.

5 **Social skills:** proficiency in managing relationships and building networks, finding common ground and building rapport.

How to use it

You can use the concept of emotional intelligence in an informal or a formal way.

The informal way is to reflect on Goleman's five traits as desirable attributes that you or others should have. Do you think you are self-aware? Do you have strong empathy and social skills? This sort of casual analysis can lead to useful insights about things you might do differently, or the type of training course you might want to take.

The formal way is to use the official diagnostic surveys created by academics. John Mayer, one of the originators of the concept, says 'In regard to measuring emotional intelligence – I am a great believer that [ability testing] is the only adequate method to employ'.

There are several different surveys available. 'EQ-I' is a self-report test designed by Reuven Bar-On to measure competencies including awareness, stress tolerance, problem solving and happiness. The 'Multifactor Emotional Intelligence Scale' gets test-takers to perform tasks based on their ability to perceive, identify and understand emotions. The 'Emotional Competence Inventory' is based on ratings from colleagues on a range of emotion-based competencies.

Top practical tip

Emotional intelligence is, by nature, very hard to measure. We would all like to think we are emotionally intelligent, but we aren't! So the top practical tip is to get multiple points of view. Sometimes you do this through anonymous feedback and sometimes through group-based coaching sessions, where people give each other candid feedback.

Top pitfalls

The problem with a concept such as emotional intelligence is that it sounds so alluring that everyone wants it. However, it takes a lot of time to change your own way of working and how you relate to others. So the biggest pitfall is to think that being assessed and understanding how emotionally intelligent you are is the end-point. In fact, this is really just the starting point, because it is then that the hard work of making changes begins. Typically, you cannot do this on your own – you need a helpful boss or colleague, or personal coach.

Another pitfall is to *misuse* emotional intelligence as a way of manipulating others. For example, if you have a really good understanding of how your personal style affects others, you might be able to lure them into doing something they didn't really intend to do. There is a fine line between being skilful and being manipulative, and it is important not to overstep that line.

Further reading

Goleman, D. (2006) *Emotional Intelligence: Why it can matter more than IQ.* New York: Random House.

Grant, A. (2014) 'The dark side of emotional intelligence', *The Atlantic*, 2 January.

Petrides, K.V. and Furnham, A. (2001) 'Trait emotional intelligence: Psychometric investigation with reference to established trait taxonomies', *European Journal of Personality*, 15(6): 425–448.

Salovey, P., Mayer, J. and Caruso, D. (2004) 'Emotional intelligence: Theory, findings, and implications', *Psychological Inquiry*, 15(3): 197–215.

4

Negotiating techniques: BATNA

BATNA stands for 'best alternative to a negotiated agreement'. Whenever you negotiate with another party, there is a chance that the negotiation may break down and that you will have to fall back on some alternative course of action. Your BATNA is this alternative course of action. Being clear on what it is, and what is the other party's BATNA, is crucial to effective negotiation.

When to use it

- To get a better deal for yourself whenever you negotiate anything – for example, a pay rise or buying a house.
- To help your firm handle complex negotiations – for example, acquiring another firm or resolving a dispute with a labour union.

Origins

People have been negotiating with one another since civilisation began, and over the years a lot of academic research has been done to establish the factors that contribute to a successful negotiated outcome in a business setting. The term 'BATNA' was coined by researchers Roger Fisher and William Ury in their 1981 book *Getting to Yes: Negotiating Agreement Without Giving In.* While the notion of understanding your fall-back position in a negotiation was in existence before, the BATNA label proved very powerful as a way of focusing attention on the key elements of a negotiation. It is now a very widely used term.

What it is

To negotiate effectively, you need to understand your BATNA. This is your 'walk-away' option – the course of action you will take if the negotiation breaks down and you cannot agree with the other party. Sometimes it is really clear what the BATNA is; however, it is not necessarily obvious. Let's say you have developed a new consumer product, but you are struggling to agree a reasonable price with a major supermarket chain. Is your best alternative here to sell it through a smaller chain of supermarkets, to sell it online or to drop the product launch altogether? There are many other factors at play here, and these include non-quantifiable things such as your personal reputation.

How to use it

According to Fisher and Ury, there is a simple process for determining your BATNA that can be applied to any negotiation:

- Develop a list of actions you might conceivably take if no agreement is reached.
- Improve some of the more promising ideas and convert them into practical options.
- Select, provisionally, the one option that seems best.

Note that a BATNA is not the same thing as a 'bottom line' that negotiators will sometimes have in mind as a way of guarding themselves against reaching agreements where they give too much. A bottom line is meant to act as a final barrier, but it also runs the risk of pushing you towards a particular course of action. By using the concept of a BATNA, in contrast, you think less about the objectives of a specific negotiation and instead you focus on the broader options you have to achieve your desired objectives. This provides you with greater flexibility, and allows far more room for innovation than a predetermined bottom line.

Negotiation dynamics

If you are clear what your own BATNA is, you know when to walk away from a negotiation. It is also important to think about the BATNA of the other party. For example, if you are trying to negotiate terms for a new job with an employer and you know there are other good people short-listed for that job, then the employer's BATNA is simply to hire the next person on the list.

The catch here is that you often do not know what the other party's BATNA really is – and indeed it is often in their interests to keep this as hidden as possible. One useful variant of BATNA is the notion of an EATNA – an 'estimated alternative to a negotiated agreement' – which applies in the (frequent) cases where one or both parties are not entirely clear what their best alternative looks like. For example, in any courtroom battle both sides are likely to believe they can prevail, otherwise they wouldn't be there.

Should you reveal your BATNA to the other party? If it is strong, there are benefits to disclosing it as it forces the other party to confront the reality of the negotiation. If your BATNA is weak, it is generally best *not* to disclose it – sometimes it is possible to 'bluff' your way to a better outcome than you would otherwise achieve.

Top practical tip

The key idea of thinking through your BATNA is that it doesn't lock you into one course of action. People often enter a negotiation with predetermined positions (such as a particular price) underpinned by certain interests (fears, hopes, expectations), and this often means that the negotiation breaks down, with both sides losing out.

Your challenge as a negotiator is to look beyond the positions initially communicated and to uncover and explore the interests that gave rise to these positions. This often involves some creativity, and some openness on both sides to broaden the dimensions on which they believe they are negotiating.

Top pitfalls

While it is useful to think through the dynamics of a negotiation, and to try to anticipate the other party's BATNA, the biggest pitfall is not knowing your own BATNA. For example, in a corporate situation you will often find yourself exposed to internal pressure from colleagues to make an agreement happen, which may mean committing to terms that are unfavourable. By being explicit on your BATNA in advance, and communicating this to colleagues, you can avoid finding yourself in an awkward position.

A related pitfall is to be overconfident that you know the BATNA of the other party. If an employee comes to you asking for a raise because he has an offer from a competing firm, do you really know how serious he is about taking that offer? Obviously you will have some intuitive sense of his preferences, and this will guide your negotiation, but if you tell yourself he is not serious about leaving, you run the risk of low-balling your offer to him and losing a good person.

Further reading

Burgess, H. and Burgess, G. (1997) *The Encyclopaedia of Conflict Resolution.* Santa Barbara, CA: ABC-CLIO.

Fisher, R. and Ury, W. (1981) *Getting to Yes: Negotiating agreement without giving in.* London: Random House.

5

360-degree assessment

360-degree feedback is a management tool that gives employees the opportunity to receive feedback from multiple sources. It is also known as a 360-degree review. It is called 360-degree feedback because the feedback comes from all around (subordinates, peers, supervisors, customers, etc.).

When to use it

- To give you feedback on your performance and your management style from those around you to help you create an effective personal development plan.
- To help the firm assess your performance, and to make pay and promotion decisions.
- To monitor the standard of leadership or the culture of the organisation as a whole.

Origins

The idea of getting feedback from different sources to appraise performance is as old as civilisation itself. For example, an imperial rating system was used during the Wei Dynasty, in third-century China, to evaluate the performance of people at the imperial court.

More recently, the German military used multiple-source feedback during World War II, with soldiers evaluated by peers, supervisors and subordinates to provide insight and recommendations on how to improve performance. During the 1950s, behavioural theorists gave a lot of attention to employee motivation and job enrichment, with a view to making work more intrinsically appealing. It was in this context that 360-degree assessment, as we know it today, was invented.

The individual often credited with its invention was organisational psychologist Clark Wilson through his work with the World Bank. The original tool was called the 'Survey of Management Practices' (SMP), and was used by Clark in his teaching at the University of Bridgeport in Connecticut, USA. The first company to adopt Clark's SMP was the DuPont Company in 1973; it was then picked up by others, including Dow Chemicals and Pitney Bowes. By the 1990s, 360-degree feedback was in widespread use, with literally dozens of survey instruments in existence. Human resources consultants began to pick up on the concept as well, which further contributed to its dissemination.

What it is

Under the traditional annual appraisal system, an employee's review was conducted once a year by their immediate boss. But if that boss didn't have a good understanding of their work, or if the boss lacked emotional intelligence, the review was often a complete waste of time.

360-degree feedback (also known as multi-rater feedback or multi-source feedback) is the antidote to these perfunctory and biased reviews. 360-degree feedback is based on the views of an employee's immediate work circle. Typically, it includes direct feedback from an employee's subordinates, peers and supervisors, as well as a self-evaluation. In some cases it includes feedback from external sources, such as customers and suppliers or other interested stakeholders.

How to use it

360-degree feedback allows individuals to understand how others view their effectiveness as an employee, co-worker or staff member. There are four typical components:

● self-appraisal;
● superior's appraisal;
● subordinates' appraisal;
● peers' appraisal.

Self-appraisal is where you evaluate your own achievements, and your strengths and weaknesses. The superior's appraisal is the traditional part of the process, where he or she offers a verdict on how well you have delivered on your objectives over the last year or so. Appraisal by subordinates is the key part of the 360-degree feedback process, in that it allows the people working for you to indicate how well you have managed them – for example, how clearly you have communicated with them, how well you have delegated and how much coaching support you have provided. Finally, appraisal by peers (also known as internal customers) can help you figure out how good you are at working collaboratively across the firm, for example by being responsive to their requests and helping out on projects that aren't your direct responsibility.

In terms of the methodology for implementing a 360-degree feedback tool, the process has the following steps:

● The individual who is being reviewed identifies all the key individuals (superior, subordinates, peers) whose inputs should be solicited.

● A survey is sent to all these individuals, clarifying that the data they provide will be anonymised. The survey typically includes a series of closed-end questions (such as, 'How effective is this individual at communicating with his/her team? 1 = very poor, 3 = average, 5 = very good'), and also some open-ended questions (such as, 'Please explain why you gave this rating').

- The results of the surveys are pulled together, and a report is prepared for the individual, giving the average ratings and the anonymised written answers.

- The individual is given the results and discusses them with a 'coach', who has expertise in interpreting these sorts of surveys and who can suggest ways of developing any weaker areas.

Most large firms today use some sort of 360-degree assessment system. It is viewed as a powerful developmental tool because when conducted at regular intervals (say, yearly) it tracks how an individual's skills and management capabilities are improving.

One issue that is frequently debated is whether 360-degree assessment should be used solely for personal development, or whether it should also be used as an input into pay and promotion decisions. While the information it provides is important, the risk of using it in pay and promotion decisions is that people start to 'game' the system – for example, by asking their employees to give them high ratings. This may not work, of course, but, whatever the outcome, the result is likely to be a tainted set of results. This is why most people argue that 360-degree assessment should be used primarily as a developmental tool – that is, purely to help people become more effective in their work.

Top practical tip

While 360-degree feedback is certainly a better way of providing feedback than the traditional top-down approach, it requires thoughtful implementation. If your firm has never used it, you should get help from a human resource consultancy in putting the methodology in place. In particular, care is needed in soliciting feedback from subordinates and peers, making sure it is all anonymous and pulling the data together in a meaningful way.

Top pitfall

As a manager, you may be shocked when you first receive 360-degree feedback, because the ratings you get from your subordinates will often show you aren't as good at managing as you thought you were. The biggest mistake you can make is to go on a 'witch hunt' to find out who gave you the bad ratings – not only is this against the rules, it also destroys trust. The second biggest mistake is to ignore the results and assume they are wrong. The results are telling you the perceptions of your employees, and even if you don't agree with their views, their perceptions are their reality and consequently impact significantly on how you interact together – for better or for worse.

So, if you receive 360-degree feedback be sure to take it seriously, and get advice from a colleague or a coach on how to adapt your way of working to improve your ratings next time.

Further reading

Edwards, M. and Ewen, A.J. (1996) *360° Feedback*. New York: AMACOM.

Handy, L., Devine, M. and Heath, L. (1996) *360° Feedback: Unguided missile or powerful weapon?* London: Ashridge Management Research Group.

Lepsinger, R. and Lucia, A.D. (1997) *The Art and Science of 360° Feedback*. San Francisco, CA: Jossey-Bass.

part

two

Marketing

A useful definition of marketing is 'seeing the world through the eyes of the customer'. Many companies suffer from an internal orientation, by focusing for example on the characteristics of the products they sell, rather than the actual needs of their customers. Marketers try to avoid this internal focus by taking the perspective of the customer in everything they do.

The field of marketing has been in existence for around 100 years, and several of the original ideas have stood the test of time. One is the so-called **4 Ps of marketing**, which defines the key elements – product, place, price, promotion – that need to be taken into account when developing a marketing strategy. Another is the **product life cycle** – the notion that every product goes through a cycle from launch to growth and maturity and then to decline. By understanding this life cycle, you can make better decisions about how to position and price your products in a competitive market.

Marketing has also moved forward, and there have been many recent advances in thinking, often driven by the emergence of more sophisticated ways of capturing and analysing information about customer behaviour.

Notions of **segmentation and personalised marketing** have developed a lot over the last 20 years. The emphasis has shifted from 'mass-market' advertising through targeting of specific segments of the market, to a focus on personalised marketing, where each individual can be targeted as a function of his or her internet usage. **Pricing strategies** likewise have shifted over the years, from a standard price for all, through differentiation according to customer segments, and now towards **dynamic pricing**, where prices fluctuate according to changes in supply and demand, often in real time. The channels through which products are sold have also evolved, and today the emphasis, especially for digital products, has shifted to **multichannel marketing**, which is a way of creating a coherent offering across multiple media at the same time.

6

Multichannel marketing

In business, channels are the different routes through which a product reaches an end-consumer. For example, you can buy a computer from a specialist retailer, a generalist retailer (such as a supermarket), online, or over the phone. Multichannel marketing refers to how a company uses multiple channels at the same time, to reach the widest possible customer base or to be as profitable as possible.

When to use it

- To evaluate different routes to market, and to decide how to combine them as effectively as possible.
- To help reinforce your chosen segmentation strategy.
- To avoid 'channel conflict', where two or more channels are offering the same product at different prices.

Origins

The notion that firms sell their products through different channels has been around for more than a hundred years. For example, the US bricks-and-mortar retailer, Sears, launched its first catalogue for direct selling to homes in 1894. As business supply chains became more professionally managed, the issue of how to manage multiple channels to market became increasingly important. For consumer products, the big challenge was how to sell directly to customers (for example, by phone or catalogue) without upsetting retailers or brokers. For industrial products, a range of different middlemen was often used (such as brokers, importers, licensees and aggregators) and there was often a risk of conflict between them.

The rise of the internet in the 1990s made channel management more complex than before, and led to the concept of multichannel marketing as a way of making the most of all the different channels to market, especially for consumer products.

What it is

Multichannel marketing is the means by which a company interacts with customers through different channels – websites, retail stores, mail-order catalogues, direct mail, email, mobile, etc. Implicit in this definition is the notion that these are two-way channels, with customers both receiving and providing information through them.

Channels are the various routes through which a product reaches the end-consumer. If the product is a physical one, it can be sold directly (such as Dell selling you a computer) or indirectly (such as HP selling you a computer via a retailer). If the product is a digital one, the number of channels is much larger – think, for example, about how many devices you can access the BBC News channel on.

Historically, different segments of consumers tended to use different channels, so most firms would worry particularly about how to sell their products through two or more channels without upsetting one or the other. For example, HP would have liked to sell its personal computers 'direct' to consumers using the Dell model in the 1990s, but they did not do so for fear of alienating their retailers.

Increasingly (and especially for digital products), consumers are using multiple channels and this is where multichannel marketing comes in. The challenge firms face is how to give consumers a choice about which channels to use and when. For example, if you buy a movie from the iStore, you want to be able to watch that movie on any number of different devices, not just the one you bought it on.

How to use it

There are some important guidelines to bear in mind when developing a multichannel marketing strategy:

- **Consistency of message across channels:** Customers increasingly interact with firms through a variety of channels prior to and after purchasing a product or service. When developing a marketing campaign, you have to consider all the different ways that customers can come into contact with your firm, and ensure your messages are consistent across these channels. Many firms have developed internal processes and technologies to support this approach.

- **Consistency of experience across channels:** You do not want a great sales experience to be destroyed by poor after-sales care. So, having established the type of customer experience you are seeking to provide, you need to ensure this is rolled out across the different channels. This includes small things such as how you address customers (for example, first name versus surname with title), as well as bigger things such as how much discretion your service representatives have to resolve problems.

- **Pool customer knowledge in one place:** Maintaining a single view of customer behaviour allows you to respond to customers in the most appropriate way. This might be done using a shared database of customer contact information and updating it in real time. Alternatively, it can be done through close collaboration across departments, or with key account managers.

Top practical tip

If you are selling through various channels, rather than simply direct to your customer, you will need to develop multichannel marketing strategies for two audiences: the end-customer and the channel agents. Both are equally important and they need to be consistent, as your channel agents will be exposed to both.

Top pitfall

Being everywhere (such as bricks and mortar, online, in newspapers, direct email, etc.) is not the same as having multichannel marketing. Use your knowledge of your customers to maximise your use of the channels they prefer.

Further reading

Bowersox, D.J. and Bixby Cooper, M. (1992) *Strategic Marketing Channel Management.* New York: McGraw-Hill.

Rangaswamy, A. and Van Bruggen, G.H. (2005) 'Opportunities and challenges in multichannel marketing: Introduction to the special issue', *Journal of Interactive Marketing*, 19(2): 5–11.

Stern, L.W. and El-Ansary, A. (1992) *Marketing Channels*, 4th edition. Englewood Cliffs, NJ: Prentice-Hall.

The 4 Ps of marketing

When launching a new product or service, you have to think carefully about a range of factors that will determine its attractiveness to consumers. The most widely used way of defining this 'marketing mix' is to think in terms of the 4 Ps: product, price, place and promotion. This is a useful checklist to ensure that you have thought through the key elements of your value proposition.

When to use it

- To help you decide how to take a new product or service-offering to market.
- To evaluate your existing marketing strategy and identify any weaknesses.
- To compare your offerings to those of your competitors.

Origins

While its origins are much older, marketing really took shape as a professional discipline in the post-war years. An influential article by Neil Borden in 1964 put forward the 'concept of the marketing mix', which was about making sure all the different aspects of the product or service were targeted around the needs of a particular type of consumer. Subsequently, Jerome McCarthy divided

Borden's concept into four categories – product, price, place and promotion – and the 4 Ps were born. Marketing professor Philip Kotler is also associated with the 4 Ps, as he was influential in popularising them during the 1970s and 1980s.

What it is

In a competitive market, consumers have lots of choice about what to spend money on, so you have to be very thoughtful about how to make your offering attractive to them. The 4 Ps is simply a framework to help you think through the key elements of the marketing mix:

- **Product/service:** What features will consumers find attractive?
- **Price:** How much will consumers be prepared to pay?
- **Place:** Through what outlets should we sell it?
- **Promotion:** What forms of advertising should we use?

At its heart, the 4 Ps is about market segmentation: it involves identifying the needs of a particular group of consumers, and then putting together an offering (defined in terms of the 4 Ps) that targets those needs.

The 4 Ps are used primarily by consumer products companies, who are seeking to target particular segments of consumers. In industrial marketing (where one business is selling to another business) the 4 Ps are less applicable, because there is typically a much greater emphasis on the direct relationship between the seller and buyer. Product and price are still important in industrial marketing, but place and promotion less so.

An alternative to the 4 Ps is Lauterborn's 4 Cs, which present the elements of the marketing mix from the buyer's perspective. The four elements are: the customer needs and wants (which is the equivalent of product), cost (price), convenience (place) and communication (promotion).

How to use it

Start by identifying the product or service that you want to analyse. Then go through the four elements of the marketing mix, using the following questions to guide you.

Product/service

- What needs does the product or service satisfy? What features does it have to help it meet these needs?
- How does it look to customers? How will they experience it? What sort of brand image are you trying to create?
- How is it differentiated from the offerings of your competitors?

Price

- What is the value of the product/service to the consumer?
- How price-sensitive is the consumer?
- How are competitors' offerings priced? Will you price at a premium or discount to competitors?
- What discounts or special deals should be offered to trade customers?

Place

- Where do buyers usually look for your product/service? Through what media or channels will you make it available?
- Do you need to control your own distribution, or even your own retail experience for this product/service?
- How are your competitors' offerings distributed?

Promotion

- Through what media, and with what sort of message, will you seek to reach your target market?

- When is the best time to promote your product/service? Are there certain times of the day or week that are better? Is there seasonality in the market?

- Can you use free PR (public relations) to reach your target market?

It is useful to review your marketing mix regularly, as some elements will need to change as the product or service evolves, and as competitive offerings become available.

Top practical tip

First of all, it is important to make sure your answers to the questions above are based on sound knowledge and facts. Many marketing decisions are based on untested assumptions about what consumers need, and often new product launches are successful because they challenge those assumptions.

Second, a successful product launch is one where there is a high degree of consistency between the various different elements. Increasingly, and this is especially true in the online world, it is possible to target a very specific set of consumers, so choices about place and promotion are now far more critical than they might have been in the past.

Top pitfall

Taken too literally, the 4 Ps can narrow your focus unduly. For example, if you are working on developing an online version of a magazine or newspaper, you may seek to replicate the 'product' and 'price' that worked in a paper-based world. However, that would be a mistake because consumers use digital content very differently, and the approach firms take when charging for online services is often very different to what worked with traditional products. Similarly, a focus on 'promotion' runs the risk of getting you into a campaign-based mentality of increasing web-page hits, when the business may benefit from more valuation content such as blogs or infographics.

The 4 Ps are a useful way of structuring your thinking about the elements of the marketing mix, but you should always be prepared to depart from this structure if it helps you do something a bit more creative.

Further reading

Borden, N.H. (1964) 'The concept of the marketing mix', *Journal of Advertising Research*, 24(4): 7–12.

Kotler, P. (2012) *Marketing Management.* Harlow, UK: Pearson Education.

Lauterborn, B. (1990) 'New marketing litany: Four Ps passé: C-words take over', *Advertising Age*, 61(41): 26.

McCarthy, J.E. (1964) *Basic Marketing: A managerial approach.* Homewood, IL: Irwin.

8

Pricing strategies: dynamic pricing

Your pricing strategy is the choice you make about how much to charge customers for your product or service. It is a key element of the marketing mix, and it needs to be consistent with all the other elements of the mix (product, place, promotion) to ensure that the product/service has the best chance of success in a competitive market-place.

Dynamic pricing is a specific pricing strategy that allows you to change your prices rapidly in response to variations in demand.

When to use it

- To decide how much to charge for a new product or service.
- To understand the pricing choices made by your competitors.
- To identify opportunities to make additional profits for your firm.
- To adapt your prices in response to changes in demand.

Origins

The original studies of pricing were conducted in microeconomics, and were based on the simple notion that firms should choose the optimum price/output to maximise their profit. Gradually, these theories were adapted to the realities of the business world. For example, by creating slightly different products at different price points, firms could take advantage of the different levels of 'willingness to pay' from their prospective customers. Prices were also seen as changing over time – for example, as the cost of production came down. And the pricing strategies of competitors were also brought into the mix, often using game theory to help predict how they might respond when, for example, you raise your prices.

The notion of dynamic pricing, while it had existed earlier, really took off in the dawn of the internet era. Internet technology gave firms more detailed information about customers' buying behaviour than before, and at the same time the internet created enormous transparency on pricing of products and services. These trends have allowed firms in many industries to adjust their prices in real time – increasing them when demand is high and reducing them when it is low.

What it is

Your pricing strategy depends on three broad sets of factors. The first is the profit targets that your product/service is expected to achieve; most companies have clear expectations about what is an acceptable level of profitability. The second is customer demand, and the overall willingness to pay. The third is competition: in an established market, your pricing strategy is highly constrained by current prices; in a new market, where you don't have immediate competitors, you clearly have a far greater degree of freedom in what you can charge.

Taking these sets of factors into account, your pricing strategy is then a strategic choice that typically seeks to maximise your profitability over the long term. A number of different models are used, often varying significantly by industry:

- **Target-return pricing:** Set the price to achieve a target return-on-investment. This is very common in established categories, such as most supermarket products.

- **Cost-plus pricing:** Set the price at the production cost, plus a certain profit margin. This is becoming less common but is still seen in some sectors – for example, government procurement.

- **Value-based pricing:** Base the price on the effective value to the customer, relative to alternative products. This is common in emerging product areas, such as games and written content online, or a new line of smartphones.

- **Psychological pricing:** Base the price on factors such as signals of product quality or prestige, or what the consumer perceives to be fair. Many luxury goods are priced in this way.

Over the last 15 years, 'dynamic pricing' has emerged as a fifth model. It is particularly common in markets where the product is 'perishable' and the available capacity is fixed – for example, airline seats, holiday bookings and hotel rooms. And it has been made possible by the internet, which gives both customers and suppliers much greater information than they had before. In these markets, you want to charge as much as possible to fill up all the available capacity. This is why skiing holidays cost twice as much during half-term holidays as in the regular season, and why airline prices vary almost on a daily basis.

How to use it

Here is an example of dynamic pricing. If you want to book a hotel room online, you will notice that the prices vary from day to day. From the hotel's point of view, the right rate to charge for a room per night is what the customer is prepared to pay. If the rate is too low, they are leaving money on the table; if the rate is too high, they may price themselves out of the market. So the changes in prices are all about the hotel trying to match supply and demand. As demand increases, prices rise; if demand stalls, prices go down again. As the date of your hotel stay approaches, the situation becomes even more complex, because the hotel realises it would prefer to sell an available room at a very low price rather than leave it empty. If you end up booking at the last minute, you sometimes get a great deal (because there is a lot of unsold demand) and you sometimes pay a fortune (because there are only a few rooms left).

The techniques that firms use for dynamic pricing are complex. They involve lots of information about prior demand levels, expectations about future demand, competitor products and prices, and the volume of products you have available to sell over what period. Pricing changes typically are made automatically using software agents called pricing 'bots'.

Top practical tip

The most important thing in defining your pricing strategy is to understand your customer's willingness to pay. It is easy to figure out how much your product costs and to use that information to anchor your price. But it is typically better to start out by asking how much value the customer gets from your product, and to work back from there. Sometimes, it is even possible to increase the perceived value of the product by charging more for it (this works for luxury goods, for example).

The advent of the internet has made it much easier to experiment with different pricing strategies, and to adapt pricing quickly in response to demand. Amazon.com was a pioneer in the dynamic pricing of books, and low-cost airlines easyJet.com and Southwest Airlines were early movers in dynamic pricing in their industry.

Top pitfalls

There are a couple of obvious pitfalls associated with dynamic pricing. One is that you don't want to become too well known for dropping your prices to very low levels when demand is low. Customers will figure out you are doing this, and they will withhold their purchase until the last minute. Many firms get around this problem by selling their lowest-price products in a disguised way through a middleman: for example, if you want to get a deal on a hotel room through lastminute.com, you often don't find out the name of the hotel until you have actually booked it.

Another pitfall is that too much variation in pricing can upset customers – they might perceive the differences as unfair and they can become confused, which leads them to take their custom elsewhere. Most firms that use dynamic pricing are careful not to change their prices too much or too often.

Further reading

Raju, J. and Zhang, Z.J. (2010) *Smart Pricing: How Google, Priceline and leading businesses use pricing innovation for profitability*. Upper Saddle River, NJ: FT Press.

Vaidyanathan, J. and Baker, T. (2003) 'The internet as an enabler for dynamic pricing of goods', *IEEE Transactions on Engineering Management*, 50(4): 470–477.

9

Product life cycle

Every product goes through a 'life cycle', from introduction to growth to maturity and then decline. By understanding this life cycle, and where a particular product lies on it, you can make better decisions about how to market it.

When to use it

- To decide how to position a specific product, and how much money to invest in it.
- To manage a portfolio of products.
- To decide how to launch a new product.

Origins

Like so many management concepts, the product life cycle had been recognised informally before it was discussed in an explicit way. One of the first articles written on the subject was 'Exploit the product life cycle' by marketing professor Ted Levitt in 1965. The purpose of this article was to argue that your marketing strategy should vary depending on the stage in the life cycle of your product. Many subsequent studies picked up and extended Levitt's ideas.

There have also been many variants on the product life cycle theme. For example, in the sphere of international business,

Raymond Vernon argued that multinational firms would often create a new product in a developed region, such as the USA or Europe, and then as it matured in that region it would gradually be rolled out in less-developed countries. Researchers have also studied the industry life cycle (that is, the pattern of growth and decline for the entire set of providers of a product category, such as personal computers), and they have studied the life cycle of diffusion (focusing on the speed of uptake of a population when faced with a new technology).

What it is

Every product has a life cycle, meaning that it goes through predictable phases of growth, maturity and decline. Older products eventually become less popular and are replaced by newer, more modern products. There are many factors at work in this process – some are related to the features of the product itself, some are more to do with changing social expectations and values. Some products have very long life cycles (such as refrigerators), others have very short life cycles (for example, specific models of mobile phones).

The product life cycle *model* describes the four specific life-style stages of introduction, growth, maturity and decline, and it suggests that a different marketing mix is suitable for products at each stage. For example, in the early stages of introduction and growth it is often helpful to put in a lot of investment, as it helps to secure revenue later on.

- **Introduction:** This stage is typically expensive and uncertain. The size of the market is likely to be small, and the costs of developing and launching a product are often very high.
- **Growth:** This stage involves a big ramp-up in production and sales, and often it is possible to generate significant economies of scale. The budget for marketing and promotion can be very

high at this stage, as you are trying to build market share ahead of your competitors.

● **Maturity:** Here, the product is established, but in all likelihood there will also be a lot of competitors. The aim for the firm is to maintain its market share, and to look for ways of improving the product's features, while also seeking to reduce costs through process improvements. Margins are typically highest at this stage of the life cycle.

● **Decline:** At some point, the market for a product will start to shrink. This is typically because an entirely new product category has emerged that is taking the place of this product (for example, smartphones are supplanting laptop computers), but it can also be because a market is saturated (that is, all the customers who will buy the product have already purchased it). During this stage it is still possible to make very good profits, for example by switching to lower-cost production methods, or by shifting the focus to less-developed overseas markets.

How to use it

There are many tactics that marketers can employ at each stage of the product life cycle. Some typical strategies at each stage are described as follows:

Introduction

● Invest in high promotional spending to create awareness and inform people.
● Adopt low initial pricing to stimulate demand.
● Focus efforts to capitalise on demand, initially from 'early adopters', and use these early adopters to promote your product/service where possible.

Growth

- Advertise to promote brand awareness.
- Go for market penetration by increasing the number of outlets for the product.
- Improve the product – new features, improved styling, more options.

Maturity

- Differentiate through product enhancements and advertising.
- Rationalise manufacturing, outsource product to a low-cost country.
- Merge with another firm to take out competition.

Decline

- Advertise – try to gain a new audience or remind the current audience.
- Reduce prices to make the product more attractive to customers.
- Add new features to the current product.
- Diversify into new markets, for example less-developed countries.

Top practical tip

The product life cycle model does a good job of describing the stages a product goes through, but it is not definitive. There are many products out there (such as milk) that have been mature for decades, and there are also other products (such as laptop computers) that moved quickly from growth to decline without spending much time in the mature stage.

So to use the product life cycle in a practical way, it is useful to think through the different trajectories a product might take. For example, is it possible to 'reinvent' a mature product in a way that gives it additional growth? In the mid-1990s coffee was clearly a mature product, but Howard Schulz created Starbucks as a way of revitalising coffee and turning it into a growth product.

Another way of using the product life cycle is to think in terms of the portfolio of products your firm is selling. As a general rule, products in the introduction and growth phases are cash-flow negative, while those in the maturity and decline phases are cash-flow positive. So, having different products at multiple stages provides some useful balance.

Top pitfalls

One of the pitfalls of the product life cycle is that it can be self-fulfilling. If you are a marketer and you see a product approaching its decline phase, you might decide to stop actively marketing it, and this inevitably will lead to the decline of that product. Alternatively, you might believe the product should receive additional investment, but then struggle to persuade your boss, who is in charge of the entire portfolio of products.

Good marketers therefore draw on a variety of data to help them decide which stage a product is in, and whether that phase might be prolonged – perhaps through a fresh marketing campaign or by enhancements to the product.

Further reading

Day, G. (1981) 'The product life cycle: Analysis and applications issues', *Journal of Marketing*, 45(4): 60–67.

Levitt, T. (1965) 'Exploit the product life cycle', *Harvard Business Review*, November–December: 81–94.

Vernon, R. (1966) 'International investment and international trade in the product cycle', *Quarterly Journal of Economics*, 80(2): 190–207.

Segmentation and personalised marketing

Segmentation is the process of slicing up the 'mass market' for a particular product or service into a number of different segments, each one consisting of consumers with slightly different needs. Personalised marketing is an extreme version of segmentation that seeks to create a unique product-offering for each customer.

When to use it

- To match your various product-offerings to the needs of different segments of consumers.
- To identify parts of the market whose needs are not currently being adequately served.
- To capture a higher price for a product or service, on the basis that it is better-suited to the needs of a particular segment or individual.

Origins

The original thinking about market segmentation occurred in the 1930s through economists such as Edward Chamberlin, who developed ideas about aligning products with the needs and wants of consumers. Around the same time, the first high-profile experiments in segmentation were taking place at General Motors. Up to that point, Ford Motor Company had been the dominant auto manufacturer with its one-size-fits-all Model T Ford. Under CEO Alfred P. Sloan, General Motors came up with a radical alternative model, namely to offer 'a car for every person and purpose'. By the 1930s, GM had established five separate brands, with Cadillac at the top end, followed by Buick, Oldsmobile, Oakland (later Pontiac) and then Chevrolet at the bottom end. This segmentation model was extremely successful, helping GM to become the biggest auto company in the world for much of the post-war period.

The theoretical ideas about market segmentation were developed by Wendell Smith. In 1956, he stated that 'Market segmentation involves viewing a heterogeneous market as a number of smaller homogeneous markets in response to differing preferences, attributable to the desires of consumers for more precise satisfaction of their varying wants'. A later study by Wind and Cardozo in 1974 defined a segment as 'a group of present and potential customers with some common characteristic which is relevant in explaining their response to a supplier's marketing stimuli'.

The concept of personalised marketing emerged in the 1990s, thanks in large part to the enormous volumes of information that companies could get access to about their customers. For example, internet software allows companies to identify where customers are signing in from, keep records of customers' transactions with them and to use 'cookies' (small software modules stored on a PC or laptop) to learn about consumers' other shopping interests. This data has enormous benefits, as it allows companies to personalise their offerings to each customer. Similar concepts have also been proposed, including *one-to-one marketing* and *mass-customisation*.

What it is

The goal of segmentation analysis is to identify the most attractive segments of a company's potential customer base by comparing the segments' size, growth and profitability. Once meaningful segments have been identified, firms can then choose which seg-ments to address, and thus focus their advertising and promotional efforts more accurately and more profitably.

Market segmentation works when the following conditions are in place:

- It is possible to clearly identify a segment.
- You can measure its size (and whether it is large enough to be worth targeting).
- The segment is accessible through your promotional efforts.
- The segment fits with your firm's priorities and capabilities.

There are many ways of identifying market segments. Most firms use such dimensions as geography (where the customers live), demography (their age, gender or ethnicity), income and education levels, voting habits and so on. These are 'proxy' measures that help to sort people into like-minded groups, on the assumption that such people then behave in similar ways. In the days before the internet, such proxy measures were the best bet. However, since the advent of the internet and the 'big data' era, it is now possible to collect very detailed information about how individuals actually behave online and in their purchasing choices. This has made it possible to do a far more accurate form of segmentation, even down to the level of tailoring to individuals. For example, Amazon sends you personalised recommendations on the basis of your previous purchases, Yahoo! allows you to specify the various elements of your home page and Dell lets you configure the components of your computer before it is assembled.

How to use it

The basic methodology for market segmentation is well established:

- Define your market – for example, retail (individual) banking in the UK.

- Gather whatever data you can get your hands on to identify the key dimensions of this market. This includes obvious information about age, gender, family size and geography, and then important (but sometimes harder-to-gather) information about education and income levels, home ownership, voting patterns and so on. Sometimes this is data you have collected from your existing customers, but be careful in this situation because you also want information about non-customers who could become customers.

- Analyse your data using some sort of 'clustering' methodology, to identify subsets of the overall market that have similar attributes. For example, you can almost always segment your market by income level, and identify high-, medium- or low-end customers in terms of their ability to pay. However, this may not be the most important dimension. If you are selling a digital product, for example, customer age and education level may be more important.

- Based on this analysis, identify and name the segments you have identified, and then develop a strategy for addressing each segment. You may choose to focus exclusively on one segment; or you may decide to develop offerings for each segment.

For individualised marketing the same sort of logic applies, but the analytical work is so onerous that it is all done by computer. For example, UK supermarket Tesco was the first to offer a 'club card' that tracked every single purchase made by an individual. Tesco built a computer system (through its affiliate, Dunhumby) that analysed all this data, and provided special offers to customers based on their prior purchasing patterns. If you had previously bought a lot of breakfast cereal, for example, you might get a half-price deal on a new product-offering from Kellogg's.

Top practical tip

Market segmentation is such a well-established technique, that it is almost self-defeating. In other words, if all firms use the same approach to segment their customers, they will all end up competing head to head in the same way. The car industry, for example, has very well-defined segments, based around the size of the car, how sporty it is and so on.

So the most important practical tip is to be creative in how you define segments, in the hope that you can come up with a slightly different way of dividing up your customers. In the car industry, for example, the 'sports utility vehicle' segment did not exist until 20 years ago, and the company that first developed a car for this segment did very well.

Top pitfalls

Segmentation has its limitations as it needs to be implemented in the proper manner. Some segments are too small to be worth serving; other segments are so crowded with existing products that they should be avoided. It is also quite easy to over-segment a market, by creating more categories of offerings than the market will bear. In such cases, consumers become confused and may not purchase any of your offerings.

Finally, segmentation is challenging in entirely new markets, because you don't know how consumers will behave. Sometimes their actual buyer behaviour bears no resemblance to what market research suggested they would do. As a general rule, segmentation is a more useful technique in established markets than in new ones.

Further reading

Peppers, D. and Rogers, M. (1993) *The One to One Future: Building relationships one customer at a time*. New York: Doubleday Business.

Sloan, A.P. (1964) *My Years with General Motors*. New York: Doubleday Business.

Smith, W.R. (1956) 'Product differentiation and market segmentation as alternative marketing strategies', *Journal of Marketing*, 21(1): 3–8.

Wind, Y. and Cardozo, R.N. (1974) 'Industrial market segmentation', *Industrial Marketing Management*, 3(3): 153–166.

part

three

Strategy

A firm's strategy explains where it is going and how it intends to get there – it involves figuring out where to play (which products to sell to which customers) and how to play (how it positions itself against its competitors). There are many views about how to define strategy – the famous management thinker, Henry Mintzberg, once identified ten different models and perspectives. This section focuses on five of the most well-known ones.

Perhaps the most popular starting point on strategy is Michael Porter's **five forces analysis.** This approach says a firm should define its strategy by first of all understanding the structure of the industry it is competing in, and then choosing a position within that industry that is most defensible for long-term competitive advantage. A related perspective that builds on the importance of competition between firms is **game theory** and specifically the notion of **the prisoner's dilemma.** This view suggests that a firm's chosen strategy is not determined in isolation. Rather, it should be seen as a dynamic 'game', where the best choice is partly a function of the choices made by others.

This competitive perspective is very valuable, but it is almost entirely externally focused. An alternative perspective, which became increasingly important through the 1990s, was to look inside the firm and to understand how its internal resources and capabilities could become a source of advantage (**core competence and the resource-based view**). More recently, attention has shifted away from the search for sustainable, long-term advantage in established markets, and towards opening up new markets where traditional competitive dynamics do not apply (**blue ocean strategy**).

All of these models are concerned with the strategy of an individual business. But many firms are actually operating in multiple businesses at the same time, so there are also some important models that help make sense of this type of complexity. The classic model here is **the BCG growth–share matrix,** which is a useful way of making sense of the variety of businesses in a firm's portfolio. This model has given way in recent years to other more sophisticated models for understanding corporate or group-level strategy.

The BCG growth–share matrix

Most firms operate in more than one line of business. In such multi-business firms, it can be challenging to figure out how they all fit together and where the priorities for future investment might be. The BCG 'growth–share matrix' is a simple model to help with this analysis.

When to use it

- To describe the different lines of business within a multi-business firm.
- To help prioritise which businesses to invest in and which ones to sell.

Origins

In the post-war era, firms in the USA and Europe had grown in size dramatically. Conglomerate firms such as ITT, GE and Hanson had started to emerge – typically they had large numbers of unrelated businesses, all controlled using financial measures from the centre.

The BCG growth–share matrix was invented by The Boston Consulting Group in response to this diversification trend. It offered an intuitive way of mapping all the different businesses controlled by a firm onto a 2×2 matrix, and some simple guidelines for how each of those businesses should be managed by those in the corporate headquarters. It became very popular among large firms because it helped them to get their hands around what was often a very diverse set of businesses.

The simplicity of the BCG matrix was also one of its limitations, and over the years a number of variants were put forward, for example by the consultancy McKinsey and by General Electric (GE). Versions of this matrix were used throughout the 1970s and 1980s, but the trend moving into the 1990s was towards far less diversification, as people realised there were few synergies available among unrelated businesses. Big conglomerates were broken up, sometimes by private-equity-based 'corporate raiders' and sometimes by their own leaders as a way of creating focus. The BCG matrix gradually fell out of favour, though it is still used today – often in a fairly informal way.

What it is

The BCG matrix has two dimensions. The vertical axis indicates 'market growth', and it is a measure of how quickly a specific market is growing. For example, the market for milk may be growing at 1 per cent per year, while the market for smartphones may be growing at 10 per cent per year. The horizontal axis indicates 'relative market share' (that is, market share relative to the market-share leader), and it is a measure of how strong your business is within that market. For example, you might have a 20 per cent stake in the slow-growing milk market and a 4 per cent share in the fast-growing smartphone market.

Each business line is plotted on the matrix, and the size of the circle used is typically indicative of the amount of sales coming from that business (in top-line revenues). Each quadrant on the matrix is then given a name:

- **High growth/high share:** These are 'star' businesses that are the most attractive part of your portfolio.
- **High growth/low share:** These are known as 'question mark' businesses because they are relatively small in market share,

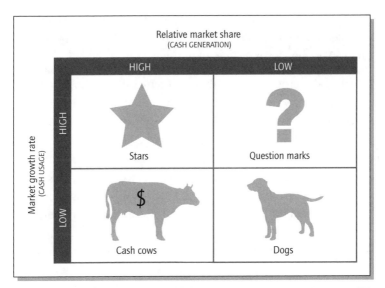

Source: Adapted from The BCG Portfolio Matrix from the Product Portfolio Matrix, © 1970, The Boston Consulting Group (BCG). Reproduced with permission.

but they are in growing markets. They are seen as offering potential.

- **Low growth/high share:** These are your 'cash cow' businesses – very successful but in low-growth, mature markets. Typically they provide strong, positive cash flows.

- **Low growth/low share:** These are 'dog' businesses and are considered to be the weakest ones in your portfolio. They need to be turned around rapidly or exited.

The vertical 'growth' dimension is a proxy measure for the overall attractiveness of the market in which you are competing, and the horizontal 'share' dimension is a proxy for the overall strength of your business in terms of its underlying capabilities.

How to use it

By positioning all your businesses within a single matrix, you immediately get a 'picture' of your corporate portfolio. This in itself was a useful feature of the BCG matrix, because some of the conglomerate firms in the 1960s and 1970s, when the matrix was popular, had 50 or more separate lines of business.

The matrix also provides you with some useful insights about how well the businesses are doing and what your next moves should be. Cash cow businesses are generally in mature and gradually declining markets, so they have positive cash flows. Question mark businesses are the reverse – they are in uncertain growth markets, and they require investment. One logical consequence of this analysis, therefore, is to take money out of the cash cow businesses and invest it in the question mark businesses. These then become more successful, their market share grows and they become stars. As those stars gradually fade, they become cash cows, and their spare cash is used to finance the next generation of question mark businesses. Dog businesses, as noted above, are generally exited as soon as possible, though sometimes they can be rapidly turned around so that they become question marks or cash cows.

While this logic makes sense, it actually gives the corporate headquarters a very limited job to do. If you think about it, the reason we have 'capital markets' in developed countries such as the UK and the USA is to provide firms with access to capital that they can invest. If you think a firm is in an attractive market, you are likely to invest more of your money in it; if you think it is in a bad market, you might sell your shares. It therefore makes very little sense for the corporate headquarters to restrict itself to the role of moving money around between businesses – the capital markets typically can do that more efficiently.

The biggest limitation of the BCG matrix, in other words, is that it underplays the potentially important role that the corporate HQ can play in creating value across its portfolio. Nowadays, diversified firms have a much more sophisticated understanding of the ways they add and destroy value – for example, by sharing technologies and customer relationships among businesses, and transferring knowledge between lines of business. The 'parenting advantage' matrix developed by Campbell, Goold and Alexander (1995) addresses these issues in an effective way.

Top practical tip

As a first step in making sense of your business portfolio, the BCG matrix can be very useful. It gives you an indication of where the most- and least-promising opportunities lie. However, you should be very cautious about drawing strong conclusions from the analysis.

Remember, the market-growth and market-share dimensions are proxies for the underlying attractiveness of the market and the underlying strength of the business respectively. It is often useful to try out other ways of measuring these dimensions. For example, you can do a 'five forces analysis' of a market to understand its overall attractiveness in detail, rather than assuming that growth is the key variable.

You should also think very carefully about how to define market share. For example, does BMW have a very low share (<1 per cent) of the overall car market? Or does it have a high share (>10 per cent) in the luxury sedan car market? Depending on how you define the boundaries around the market, the position of the business changes dramatically. Again, it is important to think carefully about what the analysis tells you and how much the result is a function of the specific numbers you have used as inputs.

Top pitfall

One particularly dangerous aspect of the BCG matrix is that it can create self-fulfilling prophecies. Imagine you are running a business that has been designated as a cash cow. Your corporate headquarters tells you that your spare cash will be taken away from you and invested in a question mark business. This means you cannot make any new investments, and as a result your market share drops further. It is a self-fulfilling prophecy.

> The obvious way to guard against this risk is to try to make a case for reinvesting in the business. Even though the business is mature, it may still have opportunities to regenerate and grow, given the right level of investment. Hopefully the corporate executives at headquarters are sufficiently enlightened that they can see this potential.

Further reading

Campbell, A., Goold, M., Alexander, M. and Whitehead, J. (2014) *Strategy for the Corporate Level: Where to invest, what to cut back and how to grow organizations with multiple divisions*. San Francisco, CA: Jossey-Bass.

Campbell, A., Goold, M. and Alexander, M. (1995) 'Corporate strategy: The quest for parenting advantage', *Harvard Business Review*, 73(2): 120–132.

Kiechel, W. (2010) *Lords of Strategy: The secret intellectual history of the new corporate world*. Boston, MA: Harvard Business School Press.

12

Blue ocean strategy

Most firms compete in established 'red ocean' markets, with well-entrenched competitors and a clearly defined set of customer expectations. Occasionally, a firm will create a 'blue ocean' market for a product or service that has not previously been recognised – a strategy that typically yields far greater profitability.

When to use it

- To understand what is distinctive (if anything) about your current strategy.
- To make your existing strategy more distinctive.
- To identify opportunities for entirely new offerings.

Origins

Researchers have understood for many years that successful firms are often the ones that 'break the rules' in their industry. For example, in the 1970s, Swedish furniture manufacturer IKEA rose to prominence thanks to its new way of making and selling furniture.

The emergence of the internet in the mid-1990s made it easier for new firms to break the rules in established industries, and it was during this era that the term 'business model' became widely used. Amazon.com, for example, competed against traditional book retailers with a distinctive business model – its formula for making money was very different to that of Barnes & Noble or Waterstones.

Many researchers studied the process of business model innovation during this period and into the 2000s, with a view to providing advice to firms about how they could develop new business models themselves, or protect themselves against entrants with new business models. Important publications were *Leading the Revolution* (Hamel), and *All the Right Moves* (Markides). But the most influential work on business model innovation was probably *Blue Ocean Strategy* by INSEAD professors Chan Kim and Renée Mauborgne. While the underlying ideas across these publications are similar, *Blue Ocean Strategy* provides the most comprehensive guide to how to define and develop new market opportunities.

What it is

Kim and Mauborgne divide the world of business opportunities into red and blue oceans. Red oceans are the established industries that exist today, typically with well-defined boundaries. Firms compete for market share using the well-understood rules of the game, but as this market gets crowded, the prospects for profits and growth are reduced. Red-ocean industries include automobiles, consumer products and airlines.

Blue oceans are those industries that do not exist today – they are an unknown market space, untainted by competition. In a blue ocean, demand is created rather than fought over, and there are bountiful opportunities for growth. Competition in blue oceans is irrelevant because the rules of the game are waiting to be set. Apple is famous for identifying blue oceans – for example, it created the market for legal online music-selling (iTunes) and the market for tablet computers (the iPad).

How to use it

Blue ocean strategy is a set of tools to help firms identify and colonise these blue-ocean opportunities. The starting point is to understand customer values – the underlying wants or needs that customers have – and to seek out novel ways of addressing these values. This can best be done using a 'strategy canvas', which lists the range of customer values on the horizontal axis and then the extent to which each value is being met on the vertical axis (see the figure below). By plotting your own firm's profile on the strategy canvas, and then comparing it to the profile of close and distant competitors, you can see visually how distinctive your current strategy is. In the figure, firms A and B have very similar strategies, while firm C has a distinctive strategy.

The strategy canvas captures the current state of play in the known market space, which allows you to see what factors the industry competes on and where the competition currently invests. It also opens up a conversation about what might be changed – it helps

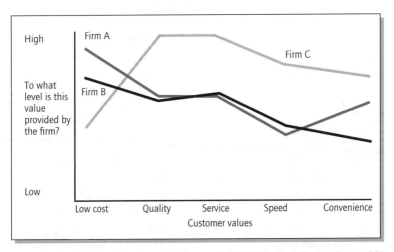

Source: Based on data from Kim, C. and Mauborgne, R. (2005) *Blue Ocean Strategy*. Boston, MA: Harvard Business School Press.

you explore areas where firms are satisfying existing customer needs poorly, and it allows you to brainstorm possible new sources of value that no firm has yet addressed. These four questions are used to guide such a conversation:

- What factors can be *eliminated* that the industry has taken for granted?

- What factors can be *reduced* well below the industry's standard?

- What factors can be *raised* well above the industry's standard?

- What factors can be *created* that the industry has never offered?

The objective of this analysis is 'value innovation', which is about pursuing differentiation and low cost at the same time, and creating additional value for your firm and for your customers at the same time. Note that this is very different to the original notions of competitive strategy developed by Michael Porter, in which firms were advised to choose differentiation *or* low cost. As a general rule, you can be differentiated and low-cost at the same time while you are in a blue ocean, but gradually blue oceans are colonised by other firms, the industry rules become set and the ocean turns to red. Once the ocean is red, Porter's original arguments about having to choose between differentiation and low cost are once again valid.

Top practical tip

Blue ocean strategy provides you with a comprehensive set of tools for analysing your customers, their met and unmet needs, your competitors' offerings and so forth. However, the heart of blue-ocean thinking is about coming up with some sort of creative insight about a product or service that doesn't currently exist. And this is really hard to do, because we are all, to some degree, prisoners of our prior experience. Breaking out from this experience involves looking for inspiration in unusual places. For example, you can look at solutions provided in alternative industries or by other firms. One useful guideline is to say to yourself 'What would Steve Jobs do?' or 'What would Richard Branson do?' in this industry, as they are both famous for challenging the normal rules of the game in whatever market they have entered.

Another approach is to make sure that the team of people involved in the discussion are very heterogeneous, and include people who are fairly new to your firm and therefore more open to unusual ideas.

Top pitfall

While the concept of blue ocean strategy is attractive, one important limitation is that the number of genuinely blue-ocean opportunities out there is small. Many potential blue oceans end up being mirages or actually fairly small markets. The process of developing a blue ocean strategy for your firm can therefore be a bit frustrating, and often yields less exciting benefits than you had hoped for.

Further reading

Hamel, G. (2000) *Leading the Revolution.* Boston, MA: Harvard Business School Press.

Kim, C. and Mauborgne, R. (2005) *Blue Ocean Strategy.* Boston, MA: Harvard Business School Press.

Markides, C. (1999) *All the Right Moves.* Boston, MA: Harvard Business School Press.

chapter

Core competence and the resource-based view

Firms don't just become profitable because of the generic strategy they have chosen. Sometimes, their internal resources and capabilities are sufficiently unique that other firms cannot match them. These models help a firm to understand and to develop their internal capabilities so that they become a source of competitive advantage.

When to use it

- To understand why one firm is more profitable than another, even when they have the same position in the market.
- To improve profitability and growth in your own firm.

Origins

Thanks largely to Michael Porter's influential work, thinking about strategy in the 1980s was all about how firms positioned themselves within their chosen industry – it was externally focused. But, to be successful, a firm has to also give attention to its internal resources and competencies – it has to have the skills to translate its intentions into action.

Around 1990 there was a shift in thinking towards these internal perspectives. In that year, a landmark paper by Gary Hamel and C.K. Prahalad, called 'The core competence of the corporation', suggested that the secret of long-term success was to understand and build on the underlying competencies that make your firm distinctive. Around the same time, Jay Barney wrote a highly influential academic paper arguing that success is built around having valuable, rare and hard-to-imitate resources. Barney's work built on some earlier academic studies, but it was his contribution that really opened up the resource-based view to academic researchers around the world.

What it is

According to Hamel and Prahalad, a 'core competency' is a harmonised combination of multiple resources and skills that distinguish a firm in the market-place. Such a competency fulfils three criteria:

- It provides potential access to a wide variety of markets.
- It should make a significant contribution to the perceived customer benefits of the end-product.
- It is difficult for competitors to imitate.

Examples used by Hamel and Prahalad include Canon's core competencies in precision mechanics, fine optics and micro-electronics, or Disney's core competency in storytelling.

Core competencies are not just valuable in existing markets, they can also be used to build many products and services in different markets. For example, Amazon used its state-of-the-art IT infrastructure to develop an entirely new business, Amazon Web Services. Core competencies emerge through continuous improvements over time, and indeed this is one of the reasons they are hard to copy.

The 'resource-based view' is a theory of competitive advantage based on how a firm applies its bundle of tangible or intangible resources towards market opportunities. Resources have the potential to create competitive advantage if they meet certain specific criteria:

- valuable;
- rare (not freely available for everyone to buy);
- inimitable (not quickly copied);
- non-substitutable.

For example, a firm owning a diamond mine has the potential for competitive advantage, because its diamonds meet these criteria. A more interesting example would be McKinsey, the consultancy, which over the years has built a set of valuable relationships with its key clients that its competitors cannot match.

Many observers have argued that it is useful to separate out 'resources', which are assets that can be bought and sold, from 'capabilities', which are bundles of resources used in combinations to achieve desired ends.

There are obvious parallels between the 'core competence' and 'resource-based' views, but they are not identical. Core-competence thinking has been used on a more applied basis, with many firms talking colloquially about what their core competencies are, whereas the resource-based view is the preferred way of thinking about these issues in academic research.

How to use it

It is useful to use a structured framework for analysing your firm's core competencies. Here is one standard approach:

- Start with brainstorming what matters most to your customers or clients: what do they need, what is valuable to them? What problems do they have that you can potentially address?

- Then think about the competencies that lie behind these needs. If customers value small products (such as mobile phones), then the relevant competence might be around miniaturisation and precision engineering. If they are looking for advice on high-level matters, the relevant competence could be relationship management.

- Brainstorm your existing competencies – the things people think the firm is good at, and the things you are better at than your competitors. For each of these, screen them against the tests of relevance, difficulty of imitation and breadth of application.

- Now put the two lists together, and ask yourself where there is overlap between the really challenging or important things your customers need and what your firm is really good at. The points of overlap are, in essence, your core competencies.

- In many cases, the overlap between the two lists is far from perfect, which opens up a number of supplementary questions. For example, if you have no core competencies, look at the ones you could develop and work to build them. Alternatively, if you have no core competencies and it doesn't look as if you can build any that customers would value, then you might consider other ways of creating uniqueness in the market, perhaps through clever positioning.

Top practical tip

The definition of a core competence is very exclusive. In other words, if you apply the criteria very strictly, most firms do not end up with any core competencies at all. So the framework provided here should typically be applied fairly loosely – it is useful to consider the various criteria around value, rarity and inimitability, but only as a way of thinking through how a competitor might attempt to beat you, or how you might sharpen up your own competitive position, rather than as an end in itself.

Top pitfall

The biggest risk with core-competence analysis is that the exercise becomes highly internally focused. It is often quite interesting to debate what you are good at, because everyone has a view. But it often devolves into a very negative conversation about what goes wrong, with finger-pointing between departments. This is why a core-competence discussion should always go back and forth between what your firm is good at and what customer needs you are attempting to satisfy.

Further reading

Barney, J.B. (1991) 'Firm resources and sustained competitive advantage', *Journal of Management*, 17(1): 99–120.

Barney, J.B. and Hesterley, W. (2005) *Strategic Management and Competitive Advantage*. Upper Saddle River, NJ: Prentice Hall.

Prahalad, C.K. and Hamel, G. (1990) 'The core competence of the corporation', *Harvard Business Review*, 68(3): 79–91.

14

Five forces analysis

This is a way of analysing the attractiveness of an industry. In some industries, such as pharmaceuticals, profit margins are typically very high, while in other industries, such as retailing, profit margins are consistently lower. Five forces analysis explains why this is the case – and what a firm can do to make its industry more profitable.

When to use it

- To understand the average profitability level of an existing industry.
- To identify opportunities for your firm to become more profitable.

Origins

Michael Porter was a junior faculty member at Harvard Business School in the mid-1970s, with a background in the micro-economic theories of 'industrial organisation'. That body of literature was mostly concerned about how to prevent firms from making too much money (for example, by preventing them from getting monopoly power). Porter realised that he could reframe those ideas as a way of understanding why firms in some industries were so consistently profitable anyway. He wrote a number of academic papers showing how industrial organisation and strategic thinking could be reconciled. He also popularised his ideas through a classic article in the *Harvard Business Review* in 1979, called 'How competitive forces shape strategy'. His book on the same subject, *Competitive Strategy*, was published the following year.

The five forces was the first rigorous framework for analysing the immediate industry in which a firm was competing. Before that, most managers had used 'SWOT' analysis (strengths, weaknesses, opportunities, threats), which is a useful but unstructured way of listing issues facing a firm.

What it is

Five forces analysis is a framework for analysing the level of competition within and around an industry, and thus its overall 'attractiveness' to the firms competing in it. Collectively, these competitors make up the micro-environment of forces close to the firm, in contrast to the macro-environment (such as geopolitical trends) that typically affect an industry indirectly or more slowly. The five forces are defined as follows:

1 **Threat of new entrants:** Profitable markets attract new entrants, which in turn decreases the level of profitability. However, it is not always possible for firms to enter profitable markets, perhaps because of the financial or technological hurdles that have to be crossed, or perhaps even for regulatory reasons. It is therefore useful to think in terms of the *barriers to entry* in an industry that make it hard for new competitors to enter. Some industries (such as pharmaceuticals and semiconductors) have very high barriers to entry; other industries (including retailing and food products) have relatively low barriers to entry.

2 **Threat of substitute products or services:** The existence of products outside the immediate market but serving similar needs makes it easier for customers to switch to alternatives, and

keeps a lid on the profitability in the market. For example, bottled water might be considered a substitute for Coke, whereas Pepsi is a competitor's similar product. The more successful bottled water is, the tougher it is for Coke and Pepsi to make money.

3   **Bargaining power of customers (buyers):** The price customers pay for a product is heavily influenced by the strength of their negotiating position. For example, if Wal-Mart or Tesco decides to put your new line of spaghetti sauces in their supermarkets, you have to accept whatever price they will pay (as long as you aren't actually losing money on the deal). There are many potential sources of customer bargaining power, such as how large they are, how important they are and how easy it is for them to switch between suppliers.

4   **Bargaining power of suppliers:** This is the mirror-image of the previous force. Some suppliers are providing components or services that are so important to you that they can charge extremely high prices. If you are making biscuits and there is only one person who sells flour, you have no alternative but to buy it from them. Intel is famous for its bargaining power in the PC/laptop industry – by persuading customers that its microprocessor ('Intel Inside') was the best in the market, they dramatically increased their bargaining power with Dell, Lenovo and HP.

5   **Intensity of competitive rivalry:** This refers to how competitors in the industry interact with one another. Of course, most firms believe they have very 'intense' competitive rivalry, but the truth is that the nature of rivalry varies dramatically from industry to industry. For example, the 'big four' accounting firms and many retail banks compete, for the most part, in a very gentlemanly way, by emphasising brand and service and by avoiding price competition. On the other hand, the airline industry is well known for its cut-throat pricing and for its flamboyant personalities who make personal attacks on each other.

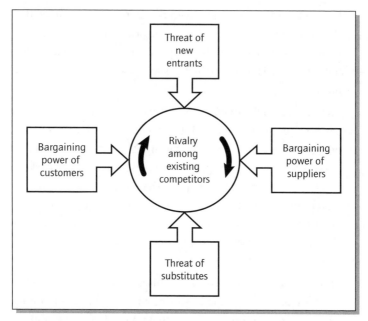

Taken together, these forces provide a comprehensive view of the attractiveness of an industry, measured in terms of the average level of profitability of the firms within it.

How to use it

The five forces framework can be used in two ways: first as a way of *describing* the current situation in your industry and second as a way of stimulating ideas about how to *improve* your firm's competitive position.

As a descriptive tool, it is useful to go through each of the forces in turn and assess how powerful they are, in your current situation. Michael Porter's book, *Competitive Strategy*, provides a detailed checklist of items to think about when doing this analysis. This can be summarised, for example, by using a single '+' sign for a force moderately in your favour, or '–' for a force strongly against you. This analysis should help you understand why your industry is relatively attractive or relatively unattractive. It also pinpoints which forces represent the biggest threat. For example, doing this analysis in the pharmaceutical industry in Europe one would likely conclude that the bargaining power of buyers, and specifically governments, is the biggest single threat.

The second part of using the five forces is to use the analysis to brainstorm ways of improving your competitive position – so that you can 'push back' on the strongest forces affecting you. For example, in pharmaceuticals if the bargaining power of government buyers is very high, one way of pushing back is to increase your own bargaining power – either by coming up with a really exciting drug that consumers start clamouring for, or by becoming bigger and more powerful yourself (witness, for example, Pfizer's attempts in 2014 to buy AstraZeneca).

Top practical tip

First, make sure your analysis of the forces affecting your industry is accurate. One way to do this is to actually figure out the average profitability of the firms in your industry, and to then compare this to the overall average of all industries (for example the average return on invested capital in US industries in the period 2000–2008 was 12.4 per cent). If your industry is *actually* more profitable than the average, one would expect to see a relatively favourable set of forces.

Second, it makes sense to focus your effort on the one or two forces (out of five) that are the most critical to your future profitability. Your analysis might lead you to conclude, for example, that the bargaining power of customers and internal competitive rivalry are the biggest threats. Your subsequent strategy discussions should then focus on those topics.

Top pitfalls

The biggest pitfall analysts make is to think that they have done their job by describing the five forces. In reality, this analysis is just the starting point - it provides an understanding of the current situation, but it doesn't tell you anything about what you should do differently.

The other pitfall is defining the boundaries of the industry incorrectly. You need to give a lot of thought to which companies are your immediate competitors. For example, this often means focusing on a specific country. If you work in banking, the relevant industry might be 'retail banking in France' or 'commercial banking in Canada', rather than just 'banking' as a whole.

Further reading

Porter, M.E. (1979) 'How competitive forces shape strategy', *Harvard Business Review*, March–April: 21–38.

Porter, M.E. (1980) *Competitive Strategy.* New York: Free Press.

Porter, M.E. (1996) 'What is strategy?', *Harvard Business Review*, November–December: 61–78.

15

Game theory: the prisoner's dilemma

Firms don't always think directly about what is right for their customers; sometimes they also think strategically about how their competitors will behave, and adapt their own behaviour accordingly. Game theory provides a set of models, such as 'the prisoner's dilemma', which helps a firm plan its strategy, taking all such factors into account.

When to use it

- To select a course of action in a highly competitive situation.
- To understand the likely moves of your competitors.
- To help you in negotiations.

Origins

Game theory has deep academic roots. It emerged from the field of mathematics, and its invention is typically attributed to John von Neumann who wrote an initial paper on the subject in 1928 and then a book, *Theory of Games and Economic Behaviour*, in 1944 (co-authored with Oskar Morgenstern). The term 'game' here refers to any sort of competitive scenario where two or more players are trying to make decisions that interact with each other.

While there are many subfields within game theory, the focus here is on one well-known type of game, known as 'the prisoner's dilemma'. The first mathematical discussion of this game was developed in 1950 by Merrill Flood and Melvin Dresher at the RAND Corporation in the USA. Because it involved two players who were trying to predict how each other might behave, its application to Cold War politics and the use of nuclear weapons, was obvious. Research in this area proliferated throughout the 1950s, with many different types of games being analysed. A key concept developed during this period was the notion of a 'Nash equilibrium' – the outcome of a game where neither party has an incentive to change their decision.

Gradually, the concepts of game theory were brought into the business world, and applied in a variety of areas. For example, game theory is very useful for understanding how firms develop strategies in oligopolies – that is, where there are small numbers of competitors who watch each other carefully. It is also very useful for understanding negotiations between individuals and between businesses.

What it is

Game theory is a way of understanding decision making in those situations where multiple participants have competing or conflicting objectives. For example, if your firm is competing head to head with another firm, the price you charge isn't affected only by what customers will pay, it is also affected by your competitor's price. In such a situation, you need to be 'strategic' in your thinking, which means getting inside the head of your competitor and acting in a way that takes its likely decision into account. The most famous model in game theory is 'the prisoner's dilemma'. Consider the situation where two suspected felons are caught by the police, and interrogated in separate rooms. They are each told: (a) if you *both* confess you will each go to jail for ten years; (b) if only *one* of you confesses, he gets one year in jail, the other gets 25 years; and (c) if *neither* of you confesses, you each get three years in jail.

This game is deliberately set up to expose how tricky 'games' of this type can be. The optimal outcome is for neither of the prisoners to confess, so they each get three years. But because they cannot communicate with each other, their best individual decision is to confess, and the net result (assuming they both do this) is that they each get ten years. In other words, maximising individual outcomes does not necessarily aggregate up to the optimal welfare for a group.

All sorts of extensions and modifications to this model are possible. For example, many real-life 'games' are actually repeated interactions between parties, so that what you do in one game influences what you do in the next game. Some games involve sequential moves, rather than simultaneous moves. Some games are 'zero-sum', meaning there is a fixed amount of value to be divided up, while others are 'non zero-sum', which means that by acting in a cooperative way you can increase the amount of value.

How to use it

The mathematics involved in game theory is challenging, and most people in the business world don't have the time or the inclination to understand the details. However, it is possible to draw out some simple rules of thumb from the prisoner's dilemma analysis.

First, try to figure out all the choices you can make and all the choices the other party can make. In the prisoner's dilemma, each party has two choices (confess or not confess) and the consequences of each choice are very clear. In the real world, you have to make some calculated guesses. For example, you could choose a 'high' or a 'low' price for your new product, your competitor can do likewise, and you can estimate the likely market share and profits that follow from each scenario. This is called a 'pay-off matrix'.

Next, you look at the analysis to see if there is a 'dominant strategy' for your firm – defined as one with pay-offs such that, regardless of the choices of other parties, no other strategy would result in a higher pay-off. Clearly, if you have such a dominant strategy, you should use it. You can also see if there are any 'dominated strategies', which are clearly worse than others, regardless of what other parties do. These can be eliminated.

These steps often clarify the choices you face. For example, if you eliminate one dominated strategy, it sometimes becomes clear you have a dominant strategy that should be the right way forward. You keep iterating in this way until a dominant strategy emerges, or the game cannot be simplified any further. In the latter case, you then have to make a judgement based on whatever other factors you think might be important.

Top practical tip

Game theory has become very popular because the principles are simple and the applications are far-reaching. For example, you may find yourself competing with certain colleagues for a promotion opportunity, which involves both cooperating with them and competing at the same time. You may have to decide whether to be the first-mover in launching a new product (and taking a risk on it flopping) or being the fast-follower. You may find yourself bidding for a government contract against a couple of cut-throat competitors, and having to make tricky choices about what price or what service to offer.

In all cases like these, the principles of game theory are useful as a way of thinking through how your choice and that of your competitors interact with each other. It is rarely necessary to do the formal mathematical analysis – a simple back-of-the-envelope pay-off matrix and a search for dominant and dominated strategies is typically all you need.

Top pitfall

One important point to keep in mind is how sophisticated the other party is likely to be in its analysis. If you do your calculations assuming the other party is highly strategic, but they end up being very simple-minded, you can lose out. And the reverse is also true – don't underestimate how smart your competitor is. A famous example of the latter scenario was when the UK government had an auction for its third-generation mobile telephony licences in 2000. The auction was designed very carefully, with only four licences available and five likely bidders. It raised £22.5 billion, vastly more than expected, and the result for all four 'winners' was that they overpaid.

Further reading

Dixit, A.K. and Nalebuff, B. (1991) *Thinking Strategically: The competitive edge in business, politics, and everyday life.* New York: W.W. Norton & Company.

Von Neumann, J. and Morgenstern, O. (2007) *Theory of Games and Economic Behavior* (60th Anniversary Commemorative Edition). Princeton, NJ: Princeton University Press.

four

Innovation and entrepreneurship

Many MBA programmes put a lot of emphasis on innovation and entrepreneurship. Innovation is about exploiting new ideas – coming up with business ideas, then developing them further so they become commercially viable. Entrepreneurship is a related concept, and it is defined as the pursuit of opportunities without regard to the resources you control – it typically applies to independent (startup) businesses, but it can also be applied in the corporate setting. In this section we talk about five of the most important models for helping innovators or entrepreneurs in their efforts.

Coming up with new business ideas is the first step in the process. A classic way of doing this is brainstorming, which is a group-based process for generating a lot of ideas around a common theme. More recently, it has become popular to apply **design thinking** to the innovation challenge. This is an approach that blends intuitive and rational views of the world, and it puts a lot of emphasis on experimentation and prototyping.

There are also many sophisticated models for structuring the innovation process in large companies. Most firms use some sort of innovation funnel or stage/gate process for sorting through and selecting the most promising business ideas for investing in. **Scenario planning** is a way of looking out to the future to identify new opportunity areas, and then using these insights to decide what new technologies, products or services the company should invest in.

For independent entrepreneurs, the **lean startup** model has emerged over the last five years as the dominant way of thinking about defining and developing business opportunities. In contrast to the traditional notion of a carefully thought-through business plan, lean startup thinking puts an emphasis on trial-and-error, hypothesis testing, and rapid pivoting to new opportunities when the original idea proves unworkable.

Finally, we describe two very important conceptual models that apply equally to both established and startup companies. **Disruptive innovation** is a way of understanding why some new technologies make it possible for startups to overthrow established leaders, as happens a lot in the world of digital media, while other new technologies help the existing leaders to stay ahead. **Open innovation** is a way of understanding the increasingly networked approach to innovation we see today. Established companies, for example, no longer do all their research and development work themselves – they will often partner with startups, and they will often use 'crowdsourcing' techniques to tap into new ideas beyond their traditional boundaries.

16

Design thinking

Design thinking is an approach to innovation that blends traditional rational analysis with intuitive originality. Rather than focusing on developing clever new technologies, or on hoping that someone has a 'eureka' moment, design thinking is an approach that involves iterating between these two modes of thinking. It is characterised by experimentation and rapid prototyping, rather than careful strategic planning.

When to use it

- To understand how innovations emerge in a business setting.
- To develop new products and services.
- To create a more experimental and innovative culture in your firm.

Origins

The notion of design thinking has become extremely popular in the business world over the last decade. It has roots in two different bodies of work. One is the pioneering work done by Nobel Laureate Herbert Simon on 'artificial intelligence'. In his 1969 book, *The Sciences of the Artificial,* he wrote that 'engineering, medicine, business, architecture and painting are concerned not with the necessary but with the contingent – not with how things are but how they might be – in short, with design'. The other is the world of industrial design and design engineering, in which designers sought to create buildings, town plans and products that blended form and function.

Design thinking was brought into the business world in the 1990s. IDEO, a California-based industrial design firm led by David Kelley, was one of the first proponents of this methodology. Kelley went on to lead the 'D School' (design school) at Stanford University. More recently, the idea has been formalised and popularised further through books by Tim Brown, current CEO of IDEO, and Roger Martin, former Dean of the Rotman School of Business.

Design thinking builds on many established management tools, such as brainstorming, user-focused innovation and rapid proto-typing. It offers a methodology for bringing these various tools together.

What it is

Design thinking is an approach to innovation that matches people's needs with what is technologically feasible and what is viable as a business strategy. It can be viewed as a solution-focused approach to innovation, in that it seeks to address an overall goal rather than solve a specific problem.

Design thinking differs from established ways of thinking in some important ways. The analytical scientific method, for example, begins with defining all the parameters of a problem in order to create a solution, whereas design thinking starts with a point of view on the possible solution. Critical thinking involves 'breaking down' ideas, while design thinking is about 'building up' ideas. Moreover, rather than using traditional inductive or deductive reasoning, design thinking is often associated with *abductive* reasoning. This is a way of hypothesising about what *could* be, rather than focusing on what *is*.

Design thinking employs a different methodology to traditional innovation approaches (as described below). It also requires a different type of individual. Design thinkers need to be:

- **empathic** – to see the world through the eyes of others;
- **optimistic** – to assume that a better solution always exists;
- **experimental** – to have a desire to try out new ideas and to see many of them fail; and
- **collaborative** – to be happy working with others and not taking personal credit for results.

How to use it

You can apply design thinking through a four-step process:

1 **Define the problem:** This sounds simple, but usually it requires quite a lot of work to get to a clear statement of the problem that needs addressing. For example, if you work for a university and you are getting feedback that the lectures are poor, you might conclude that the problem is (a) poor-quality lecturers, who need more training, or (b) the lecture rooms are badly designed and need a refit. However, a design-led approach to this problem would be to look at the bigger picture, and ask what the purpose of the lectures is in the first place. This reorientates the analysis towards providing students with a high-quality education, which may involve fewer traditional lectures. For example, it might need more online learning, or small-group tutorials.

To define the problem, you often have to suspend your views about what is needed, and instead pursue an ethnographic approach – for example, observing users of your products or services, and identifying the problems or issues they face. Another approach is to use relentless questioning, as would a small child, by asking 'why?' multiple times until the simple answers are behind you and the true issues are revealed.

2 **Create and consider many options:** Even talented teams fall into ingrained patterns of thinking, which often means jumping to solutions quite quickly. Design thinking forces you to avoid such shortcuts. No matter how obvious the solution may seem, many options need to be created for consideration. This might mean working in small groups of competing teams, or deliberately building a highly diverse team.

3 **Prototype, test and refine:** Out of this process, you typically end up with a handful of promising options. These ideas should all be pushed forward as quickly as possible, often using crude prototyping methods so that people can see how the idea might work in practice. There are usually several iterations in this step, as you go back and forth between what is possible and what your users need. Sometimes, this process reveals flaws in the original specification of the problem, in which case you have to go all the way back to the beginning.

4 **Pick the winner and execute:** At this point, you should be sufficiently confident that the idea works and that you can commit the significant resources needed to execute it. You should also have established, at this stage, that the idea is commercially viable and technologically feasible.

Top practical tip

Design thinking is a way of looking at the world that is subtly different to the traditional approach. The methodology described above does not sound radically different to what people are used to, so you have to work very hard to remind participants in a design-led project what the points of difference really are. This means, first of all, spending a lot of time getting the problem definition correct and, second, being prepared to go through multiple iterations in coming up with a solution.

> ### Top pitfall
>
> Sometimes a design-led approach to innovation leads to elegant 'designs' that are well received by users and technologically feasible, but they fail to pass the test of commercial viability. These are the most difficult cases to deal with. Sometimes it is possible to redesign them sufficiently that they become commercial viable, but if this is not the case, then you must drop them.

Further reading

Brown, T. (2014) *Change by Design.* New York: HarperCollins.

McKim, R.H. (1973) *Experiences in Visual Thinking.* Pacific Grove, CA: Brooks/Cole Publishing.

Martin, R.L. (2009) *The Design of Business: Why design thinking is the next competitive advantage.* Boston, MA: Harvard Business Press.

Simon, H.A. (1969) *The Sciences of the Artificial*, Vol. 136. Cambridge, MA: MIT Press.

17

Disruptive innovation

Innovation is the engine of change in most industries. But there are some industries where innovation hurts the existing leaders (for example, in the case of digital imaging and Kodak), and there are others where innovation helps the existing leaders (for example, video on demand and Netflix). To help make sense of this puzzle, Clay Christensen developed his theory of innovation. He showed that some innovations have features that make them disruptive, while others have sustaining qualities. It is very useful to understand which is which.

When to use it

- To make sense of who the winners and losers are when an industry is going through change.
- To understand whether an innovation is a threat or an opportunity.
- To decide how your firm should respond.

Origins

Academic research has given a lot of attention to innovation over the years. Most people start with Joseph Schumpeter's notion of 'creative destruction', which suggests that the process of innovation leads to new products and technologies, but at the expense of what came before. For example, firms producing typewriters were all 'destroyed' when the personal computer took off.

But not all innovation leads to creative destruction – sometimes it helps to support those firms who are already in a strong position. Research by Kim Clark and Rebecca Henderson in 1990 addressed this point by showing that the most dangerous innovations (from the point of view of established firms) were *architectural innovations*, meaning that they changed the way the entire business system functioned.

Clay Christensen, supervised in his doctoral dissertation by Kim Clark, took this idea one step further by introducing the idea that some new technologies are disruptive: they have a profound effect on the industry, but because of the way they emerge the established firms are very slow to respond to them. Christensen's ideas were first published in a 1995 article with Joe Bower, and then developed in two books, *The Innovator's Dilemma* in 1997 and *The Innovator's Solution* (with Michael Raynor) in 2003.

Christensen's ideas about disruptive innovation have become extremely popular, both because they are highly insightful and also because the emergence of the internet in 1995 meant that a lot of industries experienced high levels of disruption in the ensuing decade.

What it is

A disruptive innovation is an innovation that helps to create a new market. For example, the arrival of digital imaging technology opened up a new market for creating, sharing and manipulating pictures, and replaced the traditional market based on film, cameras and prints. Kodak was wiped out, and new firms with new offerings, such as Instagram, appeared in its place.

A sustaining innovation, in contrast, does not create new markets, but helps to evolve existing ones with better value, allowing the firms within to compete against each other's sustaining improvements. The arrival of electronic transactions in banking, for example, might have been expected to disrupt the industry but it actually helped to sustain the existing leaders.

Christensen's theory helps to explain why firms such as Kodak failed to respond effectively to digital imaging. One argument might be that the existing leaders failed to spot these new technologies as they emerged, but this is rarely true. Kodak, for example, was well aware of the threat of digitisation, and even invented the world's first digital camera back in the 1980s.

In reality, established firms are usually aware of these disruptive innovations, but when those innovations are at an early stage of development they are not actually a threat – they typically do a very poor job of helping to address the existing needs of the market. The earliest digital cameras, for example, had very poor resolution. For an established firm such as Kodak, the priority is to listen to and respond to the needs of their best customers, which means adapting their existing products and services in more sophisticated ways.

Disruptive innovations may start out offering low-end quality, but they become better over time and eventually they become 'good enough' to compete head to head with some of the existing offerings in the market. In the world of photography, this transition occurred in the early 2000s with the arrival of digital cameras, and then cameras built in to the early smartphones. Throughout this transition, the established firms often continue to invest in the new technologies, but they don't do so very seriously – because they are still making lots of money using their traditional technologies.

In contrast, new firms enter the market and throw all their weight behind these disruptive innovations. They often identify new

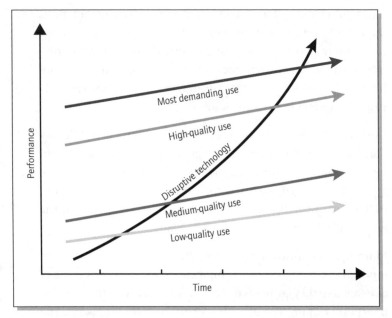

services (such as sharing photos over the internet) and gradually they take market share away from the established firms. By the time the established firm has fully recognised the threat from the disruptive innovation, it is often too late to respond. Kodak spent most of the 2000s attempting to reposition itself as an imaging company, but it lacked the capabilities to make the transition and it was handicapped throughout by the difficulty of transitioning out of its old way of doing business.

In summary, disruptive innovations tend to 'come from below' – they are often quite simple technologies or new ways of doing things, and they are ignored by established firms because they only address the needs of low-end customers, or even non-customers. But their improvement is then so fast and so substantial that they end up disrupting the existing market.

How to use it

It is obvious that startup firms like disruptive innovations, and indeed many venture capitalists actively seek out opportunities to invest in these types of opportunities. The more interesting question is how established firms use this understanding of disruptive innovations to help protect themselves. The basic advice is as follows:

- **Keep track of emerging technologies:** In most industries there are lots of new technologies bubbling up all the time, and as an established firm you need to keep track of them. Most of these technologies end up having no commercial uses, or they end up helping you to enhance your existing products or services (that is, they are *sustaining* innovations, in Christensen's terms). But a few of them have the potential to be disruptive innovations, and these are the ones you should watch extremely closely. It is often a good idea to buy stakes in small firms using these technologies, and to put some R&D investment into them.

- **Monitor the growth trajectory of the innovation:** When you see an innovation that is creating a new market, or is selling to low-end customers, you need to monitor how successful it is becoming. Some low-end innovations remain stuck at the low end of the market. Some evolve (for example, through faster computer-processing speeds) and move up to address the needs of higher-end customers. These latter ones are the potentially disruptive innovations.

- **Create a separate business to commercialise the disruptive innovation:** If the innovation is looking threatening, the best way of responding is to create a separate business unit with responsibility for commercialising that opportunity. This business unit should be given a licence to cannibalise the sales of other business units, and to ignore the usual corporate procedures and rules so that it can act quickly. By giving it a lot of autonomy, the new business unit has the opportunity to behave in the same way as would a startup company. If it is successful, you can later think about how best to link its activities up to the activities of the rest of the firm.

Top practical tip

The main reason established firms struggle with disruptive innovation is behavioural; it is rarely the case that they lack the necessary technological skills. Usually, the problem is that they fail to respond quickly because of the internal dynamics of the organisation.

So if you are worried about the threat of disruptive innovation, your firm needs to develop such qualities as paranoia and humility. Being 'paranoid' means having an awareness of all the possible technologies that might hurt your business. And being 'humble' means thinking about the needs of low-end customers as well as those at the top of the market.

Top pitfall

The concept of disruptive innovation is important and scary. However, the reality is that many low-end technologies never actually become much more than that. While you have to be alert to the possibility of disruption, you shouldn't assume that all low-end innovations will develop in such a way that they end up hurting your business.

Further reading

Christensen, C.M. (1997) *The Innovator's Dilemma: When new technologies cause great firms to fail*. Boston, MA: Harvard Business Review Press.

Christensen, C.M. and Bower, J.L. (1996) 'Customer power, strategic investment, and the failure of leading firms', *Strategic Management Journal*, 17(3): 197–218.

Christensen, C.M. and Raynor, M.E. (2003) *The Innovator's Solution.* Boston, MA: Harvard Business Press.

Henderson, R. and Clark, C. (1990) 'Architectural innovation: The reconfiguration of existing product technologies and the failure of established firms', *Administrative Science Quarterly*, 35(1): 9–30.

Lepore, J. (2014) 'The disruption machine: What the gospel of innovation gets wrong', *The New Yorker*, 23 June.

18

The lean startup

The lean startup is a new way of conceiving and developing a business venture. If the traditional approach was to define a business plan, seek funding and then execute the plan, the lean startup works the opposite way – it emphasises early experimentation and rapid customer feedback, and it uses minimal amounts of capital until a business idea is proven. Lean startup thinking has become the dominant way of thinking about entrepreneurship, especially in the technology sector, over the last decade.

When to use it

- To help you launch a new business successfully.
- As a way to think systematically about the early stages of new business development.
- To challenge the traditional top-down approach to business planning in your firm.

Origins

The term 'lean startup' was first used in the best-selling 2008 book of that name by entrepreneur Eric Ries. While the book described Ries' personal business philosophy and his own experiences working for failed and successful startups, it was based on ideas from a couple of different sources.

One was the notion of bringing the customer into the development process so that you get rapid feedback on your ideas. This approach is also used in design thinking (see Chapter 16). Ries picked up this way of thinking from his mentor Steve Blank, a serial entrepreneur and adjunct professor at Stanford University. Blank, in turn, acknowledges that this approach builds on a number of earlier frameworks, such as *Discovery-Driven Planning* by Rita McGrath and Ian MacMillan.

The other idea Eric Ries built on was the 'lean manufacturing' movement and, in particular, the Toyota production system that emerged in Japan in the post-war years. In simple terms, lean manufacturing is demand-driven, meaning that the component parts making up a product are pulled through the supply chain on a just-in-time basis. Ries adapted this concept to the startup world, arguing that entrepreneurs are more successful when they start small and build their operations only as demand starts to take off.

What it is

Lean startup offers an overall perspective on how successful new business ventures emerge. In the past, many new businesses were launched on the basis of a carefully prepared plan with large amounts of upfront investment. Such businesses sometimes succeeded in a big way (Amazon, for example), but often they failed because of incorrect assumptions in the plan, or because the market had moved on before the product or service was ready to launch. Increasingly, entrepreneurs have moved to a more iterative model, trying out their ideas in a low-risk way, getting customer feedback and then adapting their business model to the emerging needs in the market.

The lean startup model became successful in part because it captured the essence of what most entrepreneurs were doing anyway, and in part because it provided a set of tools to turn this intuitively sensible approach into an operating model. These tools have become so influential that they are increasingly being applied within established businesses as well.

The lean startup approach can be characterised in terms of three basic principles:

- Entrepreneurs generally do not have a plan. They have a high-level vision – some sort of image of the product they want to create or the problem they want to solve – and they have some vague hypotheses about how to turn this vision into reality.

- Testing these hypotheses involves 'getting out of the building', which means spending time with potential customers and understanding their real concerns. This work is best done through multiple iterations – for example, creating a simple prototype (or 'minimum viable product') that users can test and provide feedback on, so that any problems can be resolved while the costs are low.

- Being prepared to adapt to customer feedback is a strength, not a weakness. While a few famous innovators such as Steve Jobs have succeeded by doggedly pursuing their own vision regardless of feedback, the smart approach is usually to learn from feedback and to be prepared to 'pivot' the business towards Plan B if Plan A is not working.

How to use it

The lean startup philosophy can be readily translated into a set of practical tools. Indeed, one of the reasons it has become so popular is that it helps entrepreneurs to apply scientific concepts to the complex and uncertain world of new business development. The following five-step plan is a summary of how to apply it:

1 **Develop a vision:** The entrepreneur should have a clear overall view of what she wants to create, typically in terms of an unmet need in the market-place or a problem or frustration that needs resolving.

2   **Translate this vision into specific hypotheses:** For example, if the overall vision is to provide a gourmet-quality food-delivery service to city professionals, this could be broken down into hypotheses about customer demand (people will pay a 50 per cent premium over standard home-delivery services for gourmet-quality food), or operations (by serving a city market, we can prepare and deliver a gourmet-quality meal in less than two hours), or other aspects of the business model.

3   **Start to test your hypotheses (with a view to gradually resolving the uncertainties in your plan):** The key concept here is the 'minimum viable product', which is an offering that is developed just enough that the hypothesis can be tested. A well-known example is Rent the Runway, a designer-clothing rental service created by two Harvard Business School graduates. They borrowed a range of dresses and asked students to try them on and rent them out. Then they asked people to rent them without trying them on. Then they asked people to rent them based only on a website picture. By working through this sequence of experiments, they gradually reduced the biggest areas of uncertainty in their business idea.

4   **Learn and adapt:** When a hypothesis is supported, you move on to the next hypothesis and you gradually build up the business. But when a hypothesis is *not* supported, you have to take stock. Sometimes you can rerun the test in a slightly differently way and push on; at other times, you have to be prepared to 'pivot' to a different product, a different segment, or a different business model altogether. Many highly successful businesses started out in a very different place: Twitter started out as a podcasting business, while YouTube began life as a video dating service.

5   **Scale-up:** Once you have resolved all the major areas of uncertainty in your venture, you have achieved what Eric Ries calls 'product market fit' and you are ready to scale-up the business.

Up to this point, you have spent the bare minimum of money to test out your ideas, but now is the time (if you so choose) to raise money from external investors. This is also the time to build the right team of people to manage the different parts of the business.

Top practical tip

The lean startup is a useful model at two levels. Some people use it in an almost metaphorical sense, as a way of saying that they are starting small, adapting along the way and avoiding external sources of funding. Others use it in a very analytical way, as a disciplined approach to resolving critical uncertainties in the market. This is where it is most useful. The more clearly you define upfront the hypothesis you are testing, the more certain you can be about how you interpret the feedback you receive from customers. And usually it is better to work through a sequence of small experiments, rather than making multiple changes at the same time. This approach applies equally well in established companies that are trying out new business ideas.

Top pitfall

The lean startup is sometimes presented as the 'best way' to develop a new business idea, but as with all models it has its limitations. It works best in business-to-consumer new ventures where you can try things out in a small, low-risk way. It does not work so well in business-to-business settings where you are making an 'all or nothing' sale of a large piece of equipment or service. It is also not the right model in markets where speed of roll-out is key. Amazon's motto in the early days was 'get big fast'; if it had adopted the lean-startup approach to venture development, it could easily have been overtaken by a more aggressive competitor.

The biggest pitfall, in other words, is to try to apply lean-startup thinking in places where it doesn't fit.

Further reading

https://steveblank.com

Blank, S. (2013) 'Why the lean startup changes everything', *Harvard Business Review*, 91(5): 63–72.

Blank, S. and Dorf, B. (2012) The Startup Owner's Manual: The Step-by-Step Guide for Building a Great Company. Silicon Valley, CA: K&S Ranch.

Eisenmann, T., Ries, E. and Dillard, S. (2013) 'Hypothesis-driven entrepreneurship: The lean startup', *Harvard Business School Case Collection*, 9: 812–895.

Ries, E. (2011) The Lean Startup: How Today's Entrepreneurs Use Continuous Innovation to Create Radically Successful Businesses. New York, NY: Crown Publishing Group.

19

Open innovation

Historically, most firms have treated innovation as a highly proprietary activity – they have kept their development projects secret
and filed lots of patents to protect their intellectual property. Today,
the buzzwords are 'open innovation' – which is about using ideas
and people from outside your firm's boundaries to help you develop
new products and technologies, as well as sharing your own technologies with external parties on a selective basis.

When to use it

- To help you develop new products and services more quickly.
- To tap into opportunities and ideas outside your firm's
  boundaries.
- To commercialise ideas and intellectual property you have no
  use for.

Origins

As with many hot ideas, the concept of open innovation seems very
modern, but has a long history. One useful starting point is the
famous Longitude Prize that was offered by the British Government
in 1714 to the inventor who could come up with a way of measuring
the longitude of a ship at sea. The prize ultimately was won by

John Harrison, a little-known clockmaker, who invented the first reliable maritime chronometer. Rather than just hire the smartest engineers and ask them to solve the problem, the British Government opened the problem up to the masses, and the outcome was successful.

Large firms have used formal R&D labs for about 100 years, and these have always had some degree of openness to external sources of ideas. However, the approach changed significantly during the 1980s and 1990s, partly because of the exponential growth in the amount of scientific knowledge produced during this era and partly because of the emergence of the internet, which made sharing over large distances much easier. Through this period, firms experimented with a variety of new approaches to innovation, including corporate venturing, strategic alliances with competitors, in-licensing of technology, innovation competitions and innovation jams.

Berkeley professor Hank Chesbrough provided a useful way of pulling these various models together through his book, *Open Innovation*, published in 2003. Since then, studies of open innovation have proliferated and many different angles have been explored, both practical and theoretical. New approaches to open innovation are emerging all the time. For example, a recent idea is 'crowdfunding' – where an individual might seek financing for an entrepreneurial venture from a 'crowd' of backers through an online platform.

What it is

In a world where knowledge is distributed widely, companies need to find ways of tapping into that knowledge if they are to out-innovate their competitors. This can be done through any number of different mechanisms, including acquisitions, joint ventures, alliances and in-licensing, as well as more recent innovations such as crowdsourcing and crowdfunding. Companies also need to use external partners to help them commercialise their own ideas – for example, via out-licensing or by creating spin-out ventures.

The basis of an open innovation strategy, in other words, is a network of relationships with external partners who work collaboratively to develop innovative new products and services. However, it should also be clear that this approach requires a significant shift in mind-set and management approach, because companies rarely have exclusive intellectual property rights over innovations developed in partnership with others. In the traditional 'closed innovation' world, companies generated competitive advantage by protecting their intellectual property; in an 'open innovation' world, competitive advantage is likely to accrue to those companies who collaborate best, or who are fastest to move into new opportunities.

Most large companies, especially those working in high-tech sectors such as information technology and life sciences, have now embraced the principle of open innovation. This trend has been driven by a number of factors, including the exponential growth in the amount of scientific knowledge in the world, the availability of external partners and venture capital funding and the ease of sharing ideas through internet-mediated platforms.

How to use it

Open innovation is a high-level concept, so it is used through a number of different tools and methodologies. Here are some of the more popular ones:

- **Customer immersion:** This involves working intensively with customers and prospective customers – for example, to get their input into proposed new products or to get them to help design new products themselves.

- **Crowdfunding:** This uses a platform (such as Kickstarter) so that an individual can suggest an idea they want to work on, and other individuals and firms can then invest some seed money to get it started. In this case, the 'open' part of the process is about gaining access to money, rather than gaining access to people or technologies.

- **Idea competitions:** This involves inviting large numbers of people (both inside the firm and outside) to take part in a competition to come up with new ideas. Sometimes these are managed through online forums, such as IBM's celebrated 'innovation jams'; sometimes they are in-person 'trade shows', where people showcase their ideas to their colleagues. These and related models provide the company with inexpensive access to a large quantity of innovative ideas.

- **Innovation networks:** Many companies seek to get sustained access to pools of expertise outside their boundaries by creating innovation networks. For example, in the IT industry, software developers may be invited to join developer networks to help identify and fix problems, often with financial rewards available. Lego has a parallel model with its communities of lead users, who get involved in designing and improving new Lego products before they are released.

- **Product platforms:** This involves the company introducing a partially completed product, or platform, on which contributors can then build additional applications or features. Because they bring many different ideas and skills to the development process, these contributors are typically able to extend the platform's functionality and appeal in ways the company would not have thought of.

This list of approaches is not comprehensive. For example, it excludes many of the more well-established approaches to open innovation, such as in-licensing, corporate venturing and strategic alliances. Moreover, new approaches to open innovation are emerging all the time.

Top practical tips

A key shift in mind-set is required to make open innovation work, because the firm no longer owns or controls its ideas in the way that it did before. Of course, there are some industries, such as pharmaceuticals, where patents are still highly important. But in increasing numbers of industries, the underlying technology is either shared between firms or is made available for everyone to use through a public licence (such as the contents of Wikipedia or the Linux software platform). In such cases, firms create commercial value either through the speed of bringing a technology to market, or by combining freely available technologies in new ways, or by selling proprietary services on top of open technologies.

Another part of the shift in mind-set is that you cannot expect to tap into ideas from external sources without also being open to sharing your own ideas. Working in an open innovation environment requires trust and reciprocity between individuals, and a highly secretive attitude will quickly be picked up by the people with whom you are dealing.

Top pitfalls

Many firms have experimented with the concept of open innovation by creating some sort of idea scheme, where they ask people inside the firm (and sometimes people outside as well) to come up with suggestions for improvements. There are two big mistakes you can make with such a process. One is to ask a really open-ended question, such as 'How can we make our firm a better place to work?', because it will yield all sorts of random ideas, such as more salads in the canteen or a pet care facility. You need to ensure that the questions you ask are sufficiently targeted that you get relevant and practical answers. The second pitfall is to create such a scheme without the resources you need to read, filter and act on the ideas that are proposed. Without such resources, the scheme often gets overloaded and the ideas get ignored, resulting in disappointment and cynicism among those who got involved.

Further reading

Chesbrough, H.W. (2003) *Open Innovation: The new imperative for creating and profiting from technology*. Boston, MA: Harvard Business Press.

Chesbrough, H.W., Vanhaverbeke, W. and West, J. (eds) (2006) *Open Innovation: Researching a new paradigm*. Oxford, UK: Oxford University Press.

West, J. and Bogers, M. (2013) 'Leveraging external sources of innovation: A review of research on open innovation', *Journal of Product Innovation Management*, 31(4): 814–831.

chapter 20

Scenario planning

Scenario planning is a methodology for understanding how long-term changes in the business environment (such as political shifts or new technologies) might affect your firm's competitive position, so that you can prepare accordingly.

When to use it

- To help you understand how the business world is changing.
- To identify specific threats and opportunities.
- To adjust your strategy so that you are prepared for whatever might happen in the future.

Origins

The oil company Royal Dutch Shell was the inventor of scenario planning. The idea originated from the military world. In the aftermath of the Second World War, a group led by Herman Kahn at the Rand Corporation started developing 'scenarios' about the possible future conflicts that might take place. His ideas were then picked up by a team at Shell in the late 1960s, led by Ted Newland and Pierre Wack.

By 1972, the scenario planning team had put together six scenarios, focusing on the price of oil and also the likely future behaviour of oil producers, consumers and national governments. When Shell's top management saw these scenarios, they realised how different the world might look if, for example, oil prices were to shoot up. So they committed to using scenario planning as a formal part of their overall strategic planning process.

The first oil crisis hit in 1973, with the formation of OPEC in the Middle East and dramatic increases in oil price. None of Shell's competitors was prepared for this situation, whereas Shell had had some forewarning. This event underlined the power of scenario planning, and the methodology was quickly adopted by many large companies.

What it is

Making sense of the future is always challenging. One approach is to look at major trends (such as rising population or decreasing oil reserves) and to extrapolate from them. However, this approach fails to recognise that major discontinuities will sometimes occur (for example, a new technology for oil drilling or a political revolution in China), or that there are complex interactions between trends.

Scenario planning overcomes these uncertainties by explicitly acknowledging that there are many possible futures. A smart approach to planning does not assume that the world will work in a certain way ten years from now. Instead, it identifies two or three likely scenarios, and examines the assumptions underlying each one. This helps the firm to make the right investments. For example, a company such as Shell has to keep in mind the possibility that oil reserves may run dry at some point, which might mean making investments into alternative sources of energy such as wind or biofuels.

An effective scenario-planning process doesn't just paint a picture of how the world might look in the future, it also shapes the strategic decisions made by the firm and it helps them decide what sort of innovation projects to prioritise.

How to use it

Some firms, including Shell, have highly sophisticated scenario-planning teams, and the process for developing scenarios can take many months. However, you can also use scenario planning in a far more modest way. A set of scenarios can be developed in as little as a couple of days. Here are the typical steps involved.

Collect information about how the world is changing

There are many 'futurists' out there who write books and give lectures about the major trends that are shaping the world. These trends can be usefully categorised as follows:

- **Political factors:** wars, changes in government, rising nationalism.
- **Economic factors:** free trade zones, currency fluctuations, recessions.
- **Social and demographic factors:** ageing population, attitudes to privacy, consumerism.
- **Technological factors:** 3D computing, mobile technology, driverless cars.

The first task in scenario planning is to gather as much information about these sorts of trends as possible, and then to think about how these are relevant for your industry. It is often useful to gather a group of colleagues together to brainstorm about how these trends might play out, so that you can understand their second-order consequences.

Divide the trends into two categories

As you analyse these trends, and you think about how they might interact with each other, you will realise that it is impossible to foresee everything. For instance, an increased trade deficit may trigger an economic recession, which in turn creates unemployment and reduces domestic production. It is therefore useful to divide what you discuss into two categories:

● Predetermined factors – things that we know will happen. For example, it is predetermined that there will be an ageing population in the developed countries of the world.

● Uncertainties – things that may happen. We don't know for sure whether China will remain stable or whether driverless cars will become accepted.

Identify and describe the scenarios

The predetermined factors can be set aside now – they should of course be factored into your strategic plan, but they aren't important to the next step of the scenario development process. So focus on the uncertainties you have developed, and from that list identify what seem to be the most critical ones in terms of the future development of your industry. For example, if you work in the IT sector, the extent of adoption of new technologies by the population is one key uncertainty, and the extent to which power continues to be centralised in your countries of operation might be another (see the figure below).

By placing these two most-critical uncertainties onto a 2×2 matrix, you can identify four possible scenarios. You should then give each of these scenarios a name (see the hypothetical example below), and you should describe briefly what each one means for your industry and for your firm in particular.

Apply the scenarios in your strategic planning process

The scenarios are useful for many things. Firstly, they are a good way of discussing the future with the top executives in the firm and with other stakeholders as well. Typically, most people will have a 'default' future in mind that sits in one box of the matrix, and by

	New technologies adopted patchily	New technologies adopted widely
Continued centralisation of power in society	'Back to the future'	'Enlightened authority'
Decentralisation of power in society	'Pockets of opportunity'	'People power'

exposing them to the alternative scenarios they become aware of their own assumptions.

Secondly, the scenarios should be used in a more formal way to ensure that you are making the right decisions about the future. For example, one scenario for Shell might be that all future oil reserves are owned by the governments of the countries in which they are found. This would mean that Shell cannot expect to own oil reserves itself, and instead it has to become a provider of technical expertise to countries such as Venezuela or Nigeria. Shell would need to alter its strategy considerably, and it would require investment in a somewhat different set of capabilities to those it has today.

Top practical tip

The most difficult part of the scenario-planning process is identifying the key uncertainties in your business environment. It is relatively easy to draw up a long list of trends, but the really important step is figuring out which of these trends are both critical to the future success of your industry *and* highly uncertain. So if you are using the process described above, make sure to allow enough time to try out various alternatives here, so that the scenarios you come up with are the most revealing.

Top pitfall

For scenario planning to be useful, it has to be properly integrated into the decision-making process at the top of your organisation. There are many firms that have conducted careful scenario-planning exercises, only for the results to be ignored by those at the top.

Further reading

Schoemaker, P.J.H. (1995) 'Scenario planning: A tool for strategic thinking', *Sloan Management Review*, 36(2): 25–40.

Schwartz, P. (1996) *The Art of the Long View: Paths to strategic insight for yourself and your company*. London: Random House.

Wack, P. (1985) 'Scenarios: Shooting the rapids – how medium-term analysis illuminated the power of scenarios for Shell management', *Harvard Business Review*, 63(6): 139–150.

part
five

Finance

Finance provides a common language and set of tools that help managers and the owners of capital understand each other. Managers need access to money to help their business grow, and they have to make difficult choices about the forms of financing they use. Business owners (whether public shareholders or private funds) are seeking a return on the money they provide and a clear understanding of the risks involved.

Of all the subjects in this book, finance has the potential to be the most confusing due to the many technical terms being used. Once you start reading through this section, you will find that much of finance, at least at this level, relies on basic arithmetic. Moreover, learning to *interpret* the results of financial analysis is, arguably, at least as important as knowing which figures to add or multiply together.

For managers in a firm, a central question they must address is the price they currently have to pay for money (their 'cost of capital'), because it is linked to the types of returns their investors expect and therefore what types of projects they should invest in. Computing the firm's **weighted average cost of capital** will give an indication of how much a firm pays to its shareholders and debt-holders. Included in the calculation will be the expectation of returns from shareholders (the cost of equity), and from debt-holders (the cost of debt). The **capital asset pricing model** is the most widely used way to estimate an expected return for a firm's equity-holders. Deciding where best to deploy investors' money is a big part of a senior manager's job, and this is the focus of the **capital budgeting** section, which outlines the various models for evaluating investment options.

Shifting to the view of investors, **ratio analysis** is an important tool for making sense of a company's financial statements, and comparing its performance and its financial situation with that of its competitors. There are also a number of different models and tools available for **valuing the firm,** and these are important both for investors and for managers who are thinking of buying or selling businesses.

21

Capital asset pricing model

The capital asset pricing model (or CAPM, as it is universally known) estimates the expected return for a firm's stock. The calculation uses the prevailing risk-free rate, the stock's trading history and the return that investors are expecting from owning shares.

When to use it

- To estimate the price you should pay for a security, such as a share in a company.
- To understand the trade-off between risk and return for an investor.

Origins

CAPM was developed by William Sharpe. In 1960, Sharpe introduced himself to Harry Markowitz, inventor of 'modern portfolio theory', in search of a doctoral dissertation topic. Sharpe decided to investigate portfolio theory, and this led him to a novel way of thinking about the riskiness of individual securities, and ultimately to a way of estimating the value of these assets. The CAPM model, as it became known, had a dramatic impact on the entire financial community – both investment professionals and corporate financial officers. In 1990, Sharpe won the Nobel Prize in Economics alongside Markowitz and Merton Miller.

What it is

Investors want to earn returns based on the time-value of money and the risk they are taking. The CAPM model accounts for both of these in its formula. First, the risk-free rate, or 'R_f', represents the time-value of money. This is the return earned simply by buying the risk-free asset – the current yield on a 10-year US government bond, for example. Second, the asset's risk profile is estimated based on how much its historical return has deviated from the market's return. Given that the market has a beta of 1.0 (denoted by β_a), an asset whose returns match the market (for example, the shares in a large diversified company) would have a beta close to 1.0. In contrast, an asset whose returns fluctuate with greater amplitude (for example, a high-technology stock) would have a beta higher than 1.0. A defensive stock (for example, a dividend-paying utility) might have a beta lower than 1.0, suggesting its shares are less risky than the market as a whole.

Sharpe developed a simple formula linking these ideas together:

$$R_a = R_f + \beta_a (R_m - R_f)$$

Where:

R_a = the required return for the asset.

R_f = the risk-free rate.

β_a = the beta of the asset.

R_m = the expected market return.

The CAPM indicates that the expected return for a stock is the sum of the risk-free rate, R_f, and the risk premium, or $\beta_a (R_m - R_f)$. The risk premium is the product of the security's beta and the market's excess return. Consider a simple example. Assume the risk-free rate of return is 3 per cent (this would typically be the current yield on a US 10-year government bond). If the beta of the stock is 2.0 (it's a technology stock) and the expected market return over the period is 6 per cent, the stock would be expected to return 9.0 per cent. The calculation is as follows: 3 per cent + 2.0 (6.0 per cent – 3.0 per cent).

As should be clear from this example, the key part of the story is 'beta', which is an indicator of how risky a particular stock is. For every stock being analysed, the risk-free rate and the market return do not change.

How to use it

Estimating the risk-free rate is easy because the current yield for a 10-year US government bond is readily available. Estimating the market return is more challenging, because it rises and falls in unpredictable ways. Historically, the market return has averaged somewhere in the region of 5–7 per cent, but it is sometimes much higher or much lower. If the current 10-year US government bond yield is, say, 2.6 per cent, then the market's excess return is between 2.4 per cent and 4.4 per cent.

A stock's beta can be found on major financial sites, such as Bloomberg. It is possible to calculate beta on your own by downloading, to a spreadsheet program, a stock's two- or five-year weekly or monthly history, and the corresponding data for the 'market', which is usually the S&P 500.

Top practical tip

CAPM has come to dominate modern financial theory, and a large number of investors use it as a way of making their investment choices. It is a simple model that delivers a simple result — which is attractive, but can lead to a false sense of security.

If you are an investor, the most important practical tip is, first, to understand CAPM so that you can make sense of how securities are often priced, and then to be clear on the limitations of the model. Remember, the beta of a stock is defined by its historical volatility, so if you are able to develop a point of view on the future volatility of that stock – whether it becomes more or less volatile than in the past – you can potentially price that stock more accurately. Think of General Electric's shares in the 1990s, when its highly predictable earnings growth allowed it to outpace the market, versus the early 2000s when its earnings became more volatile. Had you relied on GE's beta in the 1990s as an indicator of how well the stock might perform in the future, you would have lost a lot of money after 2000.

Top pitfall

Does CAPM really work? Like many theories in the world of business it is approximately right, but with a very large unexplained component in terms of how much individual stocks are worth. Academic studies have come up with mixed results. For example, Eugene Fama and Kenneth French reviewed share returns in the USA between 1963 and 1990, and they found that there were at least two factors other than beta that accounted for stock returns: whether a firm was small or large, and whether the firm had a high or low book-to-market ratio. The relationship between beta and stock prices, over a short period of time, may not hold.

Further reading

Black, F., Jensen, M.C. and Scholes, M. (1972) 'The capital asset pricing model: Some empirical tests', in Jensen, M. (ed.), *Studies in the Theory of Capital Markets* (pp. 79–121). New York: Praeger Publishers.

Fama, E.F. and French, K.R. (2004) 'The capital asset pricing model: Theory and evidence', *Journal of Economic Perspectives*, 18(3): 25–46.

Sharpe, W.F. (1964) 'Capital asset prices: A theory of market equilibrium under conditions of risk', *Journal of Finance*, 19(3): 425–442.

22

Capital budgeting

To select the best long-term investments, firms rely on a process called 'capital budgeting'. There is typically a lot of uncertainty around major investments, and the techniques of capital budgeting are a useful way of reducing that uncertainty and clarifying the likely returns on the investment. There are several different techniques, each with their own pros and cons.

When to use it

- To decide whether a firm should make a capital investment.
- To evaluate the relative attractiveness of several potential projects.

Origins

Capital budgeting as a tool has been around at least since humans began farming. Historian Fritz Heichelheim believed that capital budgeting was employed in food production by about 5,000 BC. He noted that:

Dates, olives, figs, nuts, or seeds of grain were probably lent out . . . to serfs, poorer farmers, and dependents, to be sown and planted, and naturally an increased portion of the harvest had to be returned in kind (and) animals could be borrowed too for a fixed time limit, the loan being repaid according to a fixed percentage from the young animals born subsequently.

The first documented interest rates in history – likely used as discount rates – are from Bronze-Age Mesopotamia, where rates of one *shekel* per month for each *mina* owed (or 1/60th) were levied – a rate of 20 per cent per annum.

Capital budgeting techniques have obviously become more sophisticated over the years, but they are still based on simple 'time-value of money' principles.

What it is

Firms commit to significant capital expenditures, such as buying or refurbishing equipment, building a new factory, or buying real estate with the goal of expanding the number of stores under a banner. The large amounts spent for these types of projects are known as *capital* expenditures (to distinguish them from day-to-day costs, which are called *operating* expenditures).

The underlying logic of capital budgeting is very straightforward: it involves estimating all the future cash flows (in and out) for the specific project under consideration, and then discounting all these cash flows back to the present to figure out how profitable the project is.

There are three main capital-budgeting techniques employed by firms:

- **Payback period:** The length of time it will take for the project to pay for itself.
- **Net present value (NPV):** The net value of all future cash flows associated with the project, discounted to the present day.
- **Internal rate of return (IRR):** The rate of return, as a percentage, that gives a project a net present value of zero.

It should be clear that these are all variations on the same theme. We explain below how each of them is used. From a theoretical perspective, NPV is the best approach. However, many firms use IRR and payback period because they are intuitively attractive and easy to understand.

How to use it

The three capital-budgeting decision rules have slightly different qualities, and the best way to understand their pros and cons is to work through an example. Let's say a manager needs to decide whether to refurbish his factory's machines or buy new ones. Refurbishing (for $100,000) costs less than buying new machines (for $200,000), but buying new delivers a higher stream of cash flows.

Payback period

Here is the comparison over a five-year period:

Period	0	1	2	3	4	5
Refurbish	(100,000)	50,000	50,000	30,000	20,000	10,000
Buy new	(200,000)	30,000	100,000	70,000	70,000	70,000

If you were to use payback period as the decision rule, you can see that the manager should choose to refurbish the machines because the investment will have a payback period of two years. For the new machines, the payback is three years. While payback is not the most refined technique for evaluating capital investments, it can be effective because it is simple and quick to calculate.

Net present value (NPV)

Let's assume that the business has a discount rate of 10 per cent. Using the NPV method, you can calculate a discount factor for each period and discount the cash flows by the corresponding factor:

Period	0	1	2	3	4	5	NPV
Refurbish	(100,000)	45,455	41,322	22,539	13,660	6,209	29,186
Buy new	(200,000)	27,273	82,645	52,592	47,811	43,464	53,785
Discount factor	1.000	0.909	0.826	0.751	0.683	0.621	

The net present value is the sum of the investment and all future cash flows, discounted at 10 per cent. This NPV analysis shows that the manager should buy new machines because the investment delivers, over a five-year period, a higher net present value. This also shows how a payback analysis can fall short: it does not take into account future cash flows and it does not consider a discount rate.

Internal rate of return (IRR)

The internal rate of return finds the discount rate for the streams of cash flows, assuming the net present value is set to zero. The notion of IRR is attractive because it is easy to calculate and delivers one single number. Here is the IRR calculation for the example we've been using:

Period	0	1	2	3	4	5	IRR
Refurbish	(100,000)	50,000	50,000	30,000	20,000	10,000	24%
Buy new	(200,000)	30,000	100,000	70,000	70,000	70,000	19%

In contrast with the NPV method, the use of IRR suggests that the manager should refurbish the machines. Can two methods more sophisticated than payback period deliver different results?

Yes, because of the *timing* of cash flows. Notice that the bulk of the cash inflows happen in year three and beyond, and these delayed cash flows are penalised at a higher rate. In the 'refurbish' example, the biggest cash inflows occur in years 1 and 2. Here is what happens if you reverse the stream of cash flows – year 1 with year 5 and year 2 with year 4 – without altering the total amounts:

Period	0	1	2	3	4	5	IRR
Refurbish	(100,000)	10,000	20,000	30,000	50,000	50,000	14%
Buy new	(200,000)	70,000	70,000	70,000	100,000	30,000	22%

You can see that the IRR analysis now suggests that 'buy new' is the way to go. For perspective, the NPV analysis – using the reversed stream of cash flows – continues to suggest 'buy new' as the best option (discount rate 10 per cent):

Period	0	1	2	3	4	5	NPV
Refurbish	(100,000)	9,091	16,529	22,539	34,151	31,046	13,356
Buy new	(200,000)	63,636	57,851	52,592	68,301	18,628	61,009
Discount factor	1.000	0.909	0.826	0.751	0.683	0.621	

Top practical tip

Of the three techniques, payback period is the least accurate and should not be used unless there are other reasons why getting your money back quickly is important.

Of the other two, NPV is technically more accurate, while IRR is attractive because it provides a single, intuitively meaningful number for a given project. But, as you can see from the examples above, it is helpful to look at various techniques in order to understand how sensitive their assumptions can be.

Top pitfall

Keep in mind that cash flows are not usually invested at the same rate. Both NPV and IRR assume that any cash flows received are reinvested at the same rate. So, the first of the two IRR analyses presumes that the cash flows are reinvested and compounded at a rate of 24 per cent for each of the remaining years. In practice, cash flows received may not be reinvested at the same rate because they are used to pay off loans and other expenses, or they are invested in other projects (which may not promise the same returns).

Further reading

Berk, J. and DeMarzo, P. (2013) *Corporate Finance: The Core*, 3rd edition. Harlow, UK: Pearson.

Heichelheim, F.M. and Stevens, J. (1958) *An Ancient Economic History: From the Palaeolithic age to the migrations of the Germanic, Slavic and Arabic nations*, Vol. 1. Browse online at **www.questia.com**

23

Ratio analysis

How do you know if a firm is doing well, is an industry leader, or if it can meet its debt obligations? Ratio analysis is a form of financial statement analysis that is used to obtain a quick indication of a firm's financial performance in several key areas.

When to use it

● To compare a firm's financial performance with industry averages.

● To see how a firm's performance in certain areas is changing over time.

● To assess a firm's financial viability – whether it can cover its debts.

Origins

The first cases of financial statement analysis can be traced back to the industrialisation of the USA in the second half of the nineteenth century. In this era, banks became increasingly aware of the risks of lending money to businesses that might not repay their loans, so they started to develop techniques for analysing the financial statements of potential creditors.

These techniques allowed banks to develop simple rules of thumb about whether or not to lend money. For example, during the 1890s the notion of comparing the current assets of an enterprise to its current liabilities (known as the 'current ratio') was developed. Gradually, these methods became more sophisticated, and now there are dozens of different ratios that analysts keep track of.

What it is

There are four main categories of financial ratios. Consider the following financial results for three global firms in the smartphone industry:

	Firm A	Firm B	Firm C
Net sales	217,462	170,910	17,497
Cost of sales	130,934	106,606	10,138
Gross margin	86,528	64,304	7,359
Net income (loss)	28,978	37,037	(1,017)
Total shareholders' equity	142,649	123,549	9,169
Accounts receivable, net	23,761	13,102	3,994
Accounts payable	1,002	22,367	2,536
Inventories	18,195	1,764	1,107
Land and buildings	71,789	3,309	779
Cash equivalents	57,751	146,761	5,061
Total assets	203,562	207,000	34,681

Looking at the raw figures, we can see that Firm A has the highest sales, Firm B has the highest net income (among other marketing leading figures) and Firm C has the lowest level of inventory relative to its sales. In order to compare one firm's results against another's, the creation of common, standardised ratios is needed. The four major categories of ratios are as follows:

1　**Profit sustainability:** How well is your firm performing over a specific period? Will it have the financial resources to continue serving its customers tomorrow as well as today? Useful ratios here are: sales growth (sales for current period/sales for previous period), return on assets (net profit/total assets) and return on equity (net profit/shareholders' equity).

2   **Operational efficiency:** How efficiently are you utilising your assets and managing your liabilities? These ratios are used to compare performance over multiple periods. Examples include: inventory turns (sales/cost of inventory), days receivable (accounts receivable/[sales/365]) and days payable (accounts payable/[cost of goods sold/365]).

3   **Liquidity:** Does your firm have enough cash on an ongoing basis to meet its operational obligations? This is an important indication of financial health. Key ratios here are: current ratio (current assets/current liabilities) and quick ratio (cash + marketable securities + accounts receivable/current liabilities).

4   **Leverage (also known as gearing):** To what degree does your firm utilise borrowed money and what is its level of risk? Lenders often use this information to determine a firm's ability to repay debt. Examples are: debt-to-equity ratio (debt/equity) and interest coverage (EBIT/interest expense).

These are some of the standard ratios used in business practice and are provided as guidelines. Not all these ratios will provide the information you need to support your particular decisions and strategies; you can also develop your own ratios and indicators based on what you consider important and meaningful to your firm.

How to use it

By comparing the ratio of a figure – or a combination of figures – to another figure, trends can be observed. Using just the data from the table below, the following ratios can be created:

	Firm A	Firm B	Firm C
Inventory turns	7.2	60.4	9.2
Days inventory	50.7	6.0	39.9
Days receivable	39.9	28.0	83.3
Days payable	2.8	76.6	91.3
ROA	14.2%	17.9%	−2.9%
ROA, excluding cash and cash equivalents	19.9%	61.5%	−3.4%
ROE	20.3%	30.0%	−11.1%

You can see that while Firm A is generating the most revenue, Firm B is likely to be an industry leader because it is very liquid, efficient and profitable. Having this standardised set of ratios allows managers to make better decisions – for example, which firms to invest in and which firms to monitor. Shareholders also use ratios to understand how their firms are performing versus their peers.

Top practical tip

Make sure to calculate a number of different ratios to ensure you get an accurate picture. Each ratio gives some insight, but the more you have, the more rounded your view becomes. And as with all forms of financial analysis, ratios don't provide the 'answer' as to why a firm is performing well or badly – they are simply a way of homing in on the key questions that need to be answered in a more considered way.

Top pitfall

For ratios to be meaningful they need to be based on accurate financial information, otherwise you run the risk of falling into the 'garbage in–garbage out' trap. One key mistake is comparing fiscal year results for a number of comparable firms but failing to recognise that firms have different fiscal year-ends (some are at the end of January, others have a year-end in June). Ratios also are only really meaningful when used in a comparative way – for example, looking at how a set of ratios changes over time in the same firm, or how a number of competing firms have very different ratios.

Further reading

McKenzie, W. (2013) *FT Guide to Using and Interpreting Company Accounts*, 4th edition. Upper Saddle River, NJ: FT Press/Prentice Hall.

Ormiston, A.M. and Fraser, L.M. (2012) *Understanding Financial Statements*, 10th edition. Harlow, UK: Pearson Education.

chapter

24

Valuing the firm

What is a firm worth? Answering this question will allow you to
determine if it is undervalued or overvalued compared to its peers.
Unfortunately, there is no single model for analysing what a firm is
worth. Here, we describe four different models and we explain the
pros and cons of each one.

When to use it

- To decide the right price when making an acquisition.
- To defend your own company against an acquisition.
- As an investor, to decide when to buy or sell shares in a firm.

Origins

Managers and investors have needed to value firms for as long as
there have been firms to buy or stocks to invest in. Early attempts at
valuation focused on simple analysis of cash flows and profitability.
As the notion of 'time-value of money' became understood, valuation methods started to incorporate discount rates and they also
considered how a company was financed.

In a review of the use of discounted cash flow in history, R.H. Parker (1968) notes that the earliest interest-rate tables date back to 1340 and were prepared by Francesco Balducci Pegolotti, a Florentine merchant and politician. The development of insurance and actuarial sciences in the next few centuries provided an impetus for a more thorough study of present value. Simon Stevin, a Flemish mathematician, wrote one of the first textbooks on financial mathematics in 1582, in which he laid out the basis for the present value rule.

What it is

Firm-valuation methods all involve analysing a firm's financial statements and coming up with an estimate of what the firm is ultimately worth. There are absolute methods, which hone in on the firm's ability to generate cash and its cost of capital, and there are relative methods, which compare a firm's performance with that of its peer group. Be aware that the estimate of a firm's value will change depending on the technique being used and the assumptions the analyst has selected.

How to use it

The basic question that investors ask is this: 'Is the firm undervalued or overvalued relative to its stock price?'. Here, we illustrate four firm-valuation techniques:

1 **Asset-based valuation** – based solely on its balance sheet.
2 **Comparable transaction valuation** – when compared to its peer group.

3 **Discounted cash flow** – given its stream of future cash flows and its cost of capital.

4 **Dividend discount model** – given the dividend stream it intends to return to investors.

Let's work through an example to see how the four valuation methods are put into practice. Here we have a firm, Luxury Desserts, which produces high-end desserts for the New York City market. It has historical results from 2013 to 2015 and projected results over the next five years (all figures in thousands – see table below).

One can see that this firm intends to grow its revenues rapidly. While net income is expected to grow, net margin is anticipated to remain about the same. Looking at Luxury Dessert's balance sheets for the past few years (below), we can see that the firm's retained earnings have increased, and it is carrying about half-a-million in cash on its books. We have also compiled a set of dessert companies that are similar to Luxury Desserts (below). We will use this set of comparators in our analysis.

Note that one of the firms, Sunrise Treats, has significantly higher sales than the rest of the comparators.

Asset-based valuation

This technique looks at the fair-market value of the company's equity, which is calculated by deducting total liabilities from total assets. The focus is on the fair-market value of its total assets minus total liabilities. According to basic accounting principles, a firm's income statement provides a measure of its true earnings potential, while the balance sheet gives a reliable estimate of the value of the assets and equity in the firm.

Luxury Desserts: recent and projected income statements

Income statement	2013	2014	2015	2016 F	2017 F	2018 F	2019 F	2020 F
Revenue	$4,407	$5,244	$5,768	$7,822	$9,878	$12,442	$14,654	$17,161
Labour	$1,763	$2,045	$2,192					
Materials	$1,542	$1,730	$1,904					
Gross margin	$1,102	$1,468	$1,673	$2,212	$2,693	$3,283	$3,856	$4,518
Total other expenses	$686	$815	$960	$1,173	$1,482	$1,866	$2,198	$2,574
EBITDA	$415	$654	$713	$1,038	$1,212	$1,416	$1,658	$1,944
Amortisation	$103	$107	$112	$115	$169	$172	$175	$177
Interest expense	$18	$18	$18	$160	$160	$160	$160	$160
EBT	$295	$528	$583	$763	$883	$1,084	$1,323	$1,607
Tax (38%)	$112	$201	$222	$290	$335	$412	$503	$611
Net income	$183	$328	$361	$473	$547	$672	$820	$996
Net margin	4.2%	6.2%	6.3%	6.0%	5.5%	5.4%	5.6%	5.8%

Luxury Desserts: balance sheets

Balance sheet	2013	2014	2015
Assets			
Cash	$76	$249	$546
Accounts receivable	$749	$813	$808
Prepaid expenses	$110	$131	$144
Inventory	$220	$247	$293
Fixed assets	$1,073	$1,115	$1,154
	$2,228	$2,555	$2,944
Liabilities and equity			
Operating line	$–	$–	$–
Accounts payable	$278	$277	$305
Long-term debt	$200	$200	$200
	$478	$477	$505
Contributed equity	$250	$250	$250
Retained earnings	$1,501	$1,828	$2,190
	$2,228	$2,555	$2,944

Luxury Desserts: comparable firms

Target company	2015 Sales	EBITDA	Target price
Artisan Cakes	$12,000	$1,300	$7,800
Italian Bakery	$2,200	$350	$1,225
Wedding Cake Suppliers	$3,000	$600	$2,700
Sunrise Treats	$35,000	$3,000	$36,000
Meadow Breads	$6,000	$750	$3,000

In Luxury Desserts' case, total assets are $2,944,000 and total liabilities are $505,000, leaving net asset value, or equity, of $2,440,000. If we assume the market value of equity is the same as the net asset value, then Luxury Desserts is worth just under $2.5 million. This is one way of valuing a firm, but – as we will see – it is typically an *underestimate* of value because there are some assets (such as loyal customers or the power of a brand) that are not put on the balance sheet.

Comparable transaction valuation

The second valuation method looks for comparable firms to see how much they are trading for on the stock market. When you want to sell your home, you estimate its value by looking at how much a similar house down the street sold for, and this is the same principle.

The challenge here is identifying the right comparison firms. Ideally, a comparable firm is one that is quite similar – a direct competitor in the same industry – but of course it is very difficult to find firms that are so well matched. In practice, most analysts start by comparing the firm being valued to four or five of the closest competitors in its industry sector. If there are more than a handful of candidates, the analyst can focus on firms of similar size and growth potential. For example, in the smartphone industry, an analyst might compare Apple Inc. to Samsung as both are market leaders, but exclude Sony's entry, assuming financials can be broken out for the latter unit.

We have five comparators for this valuation exercise. Dividing the target price by EBITDA, we arrive at what multiple of EBITDA each firm is worth:

Target company	2015 Sales	EBITDA	Target price	EBITDA multiple
Artisan Cakes	$12,000	$1,300	$7,800	6.0×
Italian Bakery	$2,200	$350	$1,225	3.5×
Wedding Cake Supplies	$3,000	$600	$2,700	4.5×
Sunrise Treats	$35,000	$3,000	$36,000	12.0×
Meadow Breads	$6,000	$750	$3,000	4.0×
Average				6.0×
Average excluding Sunrise Treats				4.5×

Notice that the average is computed both with and without Sunrise Treats. Because Sunrise Treats is significantly larger than the rest of the firms, one can argue for an exclusion of Sunrise Treats in the analysis. Given that Luxury Desserts had 2015 EBITDA of $713,000, we can estimate the value of Luxury Desserts based on the comparable transactions analysis (000s):

		2015 EBITDA	Implied value
Average	6.0×	$713	$4,275
Average excluding Sunrise Treats	4.5×	$713	$3,206

Depending on the comparator set used, Luxury Desserts is estimated to be worth $3,206,000 or $4,275,000. We have used a multiple of EBITDA in our comparable transactions analysis. Other multiples may be used in combination or in place of a multiple of EBITDA. These include earnings multiples and sales multiples, to cite two examples.

Discounted cash flow (DCF)

The DCF analysis is based on the observation that the value of the firm is linked to how much free cash flow it can generate. These cash flows are discounted back to present value using the firm's discount rate. The firm's discount rate is its cost of capital, which includes what its shareholders expected to earn on equity and what its debt-holders are owed on its debt.

The typical DCF calculation discounts a firm's 'unlevered free cash flow' (UFCF) by a discount rate to get to the present value of the projected results. UFCF simply means the firm's cash flows before it makes interest payments – hence the use of the term 'unlevered' in the metric.

Let's look at Luxury Dessert's example:

DCF	2016 F	2017 F	2018 F	2019 F	2020 F
Unlevered free cash flow (UFCF)					
Revenue	$7,821.8	$9,877.8	$12,442.1	$14,654.1	$17,160.9
EBITDA	$1,038.3	$1,211.7	$1,416.3	$1,658.1	$1,944.1
less: Amortisation	−$115.4	−$168.8	−$172.0	−$174.8	−$177.3
EBIT	$922.9	$1,042.8	$1,244.4	$1,483.4	$1,766.9
less: Tax (38%)	−$350.7	−$396.3	−$472.9	−$563.7	−$671.4
EBIAT	$572.2	$646.6	$771.5	$919.7	$1,095.4
EBIAT	$572.2	$646.6	$771.5	$919.7	$1,095.4
add: Amortisation	$115.4	$168.8	$172.0	$174.8	$177.3
less: Capex	−$650.0	−$200.0	−$200.0	−$200.0	−$200.0
less: Working capital investment	−$150.0	−$150.0	−$150.0	−$150.0	−$150.0
UFCF (unlevered free cash flow)	−$112.4	$465.4	$593.5	$744.4	$922.7

Note that the calculation starts with EBITDA, removes amortisation (the 'DA'), then calculates the tax on EBIT (remember that this is a firm's 'unlevered' cash flow calculation). The result is EBIAT, or earnings before interest but after tax. Then amortisation, which is a non-cash expense, is added back, and cash expenses for capital expenditures and any investments in working capital are deducted. The result is UFCF.

Let's assume the weighted average cost of capital (WACC) for our discount rate is 18 per cent. Using the assumed WACC, we find that the present value of Luxury Desserts' UFCF is $1,406,000 (see table below).

Don't miss out on an important step in this exercise: determining the terminal value of the firm. The tricky thing is that Luxury Desserts is expected to continue operating after the fifth year

Net present value of UFCF	2016 F	2017 F	2018 F	2019 F	2020 F
Period	1	2	3	4	5
Discount factor	0.85	0.72	0.61	0.52	0.44
PV of UFCF	−$95.3	$334.2	$361.2	$384.0	$403.3
Total PV of UFCF					$1,387.5

(2020). In calculating a terminal value for the UFCFs before 2020, we can assume a perpetual growth rate (g) of 4.0 per cent, and the same WACC of 18 per cent. The formula for terminal value is:

$$\frac{UFCF_n \times (1 + g)}{WACC - g}$$

Thus, the terminal value for Luxury Desserts at the end of 2020 is*:

$$\frac{923 \times (1 + 4.0\%)}{18.0\% - 4.0\%} = 6,856,571$$

We find the present value of this terminal value by multiplying $6,856,571 by 0.44 (it's 0.4371 before rounding) to get $2,997,007. In the previous example, 0.44 is the discount factor for 2020, or the end of the fifth year. Note that the present value of the terminal value is much higher than the present value of the five years of cash flows. This is why it is important to remember to estimate a terminal value in the first place.

We add the present value of the UFCFs ($1,387,458) to the present value of the terminal value ($2,997,007) to get Luxury Desserts' DCF value of $4,384,465.

Dividend discount model

This method simply looks at the cash to be received by shareholders. Investors look either for capital gains (think high-tech 'Unicorns' or startups worth more than $1 billion, many of which have

---

*A reminder: rounded values are used here only for presentation purposes.

never turned a profit), or for dividends (for example, telecommunications and utilities).

This model works best when dividends are known, are steady and are expected to grow at a predictable rate. The simplest version of the dividend discount model, the 'Gordon growth model', can be used to value a firm that is in 'steady state' with dividends growing at a rate that can be sustained forever. The Gordon growth model relates the value of a stock to its expected dividends in the next time period, the cost of equity and the expected growth rate in dividends.

$$\text{Value of stock} = \frac{\text{DPS}_1}{k_e - g}$$

Where:

DPS$_1$ = the expected dividend one period from now.

k_e = the required rate of return for equity holders.

g = the perpetual annual growth rate for the dividend.

Using Luxury Desserts' example, let's assume investors can expect dividends of $400,000 per year, growing at rate of 15 per cent a year in perpetuity:

Expected dividend one period from now	400
Required rate of return for equity holders	26%
Perpetual annual growth rate for the dividend	15%
	$3,636

In this case, Luxury Desserts is worth $3,636,000.

In summary, the various valuation methods yield different results due to the different inputs used in the calculations:

● Asset-based valuation: $2,440,000.

● Comparable transaction valuation: $3,206,000 to $4,275,000.

● Discounted cash flow: $4,384,465.

● Dividend discount model: $3,636,000.

Clearly there is no single right answer to the question, 'What is Luxury Desserts worth?'. This analysis provides a range of estimates (from $2.4m to $4.4m), and as an analyst or potential investor you would now be expected to consider various subjective factors to come to an opinion on what number is most realistic. Some of these factors are about the intangible strengths and weaknesses of the firm – for example, how loyal its customers are, or how skilled you consider the firm's managers to be. Equally important are external factors, such as how volatile the market is or whether new competitors are emerging.

Finally, you also have to consider how strongly the current owners of the firm want to sell, and whether other buyers are out there. Such factors often result in a much higher price being paid than would be expected using these valuation methods.

Top practical tip

For valuation analysis to be useful and meaningful, make sure to use several techniques as part of your due diligence process. They will always yield slightly different results, and these differences help you to build a more complete picture of the firm you are valuing. It is also important to understand the mechanics behind your calculations, to get a sense for which inputs are the most heavily weighted.

Top pitfall

The biggest mistake in valuation analysis is to assume that the calculations are 'right'. Remember, all these techniques are based on assumptions. So learn to be critical about the inputs you are given, as a small change (such as the assumed growth rate) can have a large impact on the final valuation.

Further reading

Berk, J. and DeMarzo, P. (2013) *Corporate Finance: The core.* Harlow, UK: Pearson.

Gordon, M.J. and Shapiro, E. (1956) 'Capital equipment analysis: The required rate of profit', *Management Science,* 3(1): 102–110.

Parker, R.H. (1968) *Discounted Cash Flow in Historical Perspective.* Chicago, IL: Institute of Professional Accounting.

chapter 25

Weighted average cost of capital

A firm's 'weighted average cost of capital' (or WACC) is a financial metric used to measure the cost of capital to a firm. It is a weighted average of the firm's cost of debt and its cost of equity.

When to use it

- To decide what discount rate to use in capital budgeting decisions.
- To evaluate potential investments.

Origins

The term 'cost of capital' was first used in an academic study by Ferry Allen in 1954: he discussed how different proportions of equity and debt would result in higher or lower costs of capital, so it was important for managers to find the right balance.

However, this informal analysis was eclipsed by Modigliani and Miller's seminal paper, 'The cost of capital, corporation finance and the theory of investment', published in 1958. This paper provided a strong theoretical foundation to discussions about the right capital structure in firms. Building on this theory, the WACC formula is a straightforward way of calculating the approximate overall cost of capital for a specific firm.

What it is

Firms are generally financed through two methods – through debt, which means borrowing money from lenders, and through equity, which means selling a stake in the firm to investors. There is a cost to both these financing methods. Holders of debt expect to receive interest on their loan. Holders of equity expect their share in the firm to go up in value, and may receive an annual dividend payment.

The weighted average cost of capital for a firm is calculated by working out the cost of debt (which is simply a function of the interest rate it pays) and the cost of its equity (a more complicated formula, as described below), and then coming up with a weighted average of the two depending on its proportions of debt and equity.

In more technical terms, the WACC equation is the cost of each capital component multiplied by its proportional weight and then summing:

$$\text{WACC} = \frac{E}{V} \times R_e + \frac{D}{V} \times R_d \times (1 - T_c)$$

Where:

R_e = the cost of equity.

R_d = the cost of debt.

E = the market value of the firm's equity.

D = the market value of the firm's debt.

$V = E + D$ = the total market value of all sources of financing (both equity and debt) in the firm.

$\dfrac{E}{V}$ = the percentage of total financing that is equity.

$\dfrac{D}{V}$ = the percentage of total financing that is debt.

T_c = the corporate tax rate.

In summary, WACC is an aggregate measure of the cost the firm incurs in using funds of creditors and shareholders. This measure has implications for those running the firm and for potential investors. For those running the firm, creating value requires investing in capital projects that provide a return greater than the WACC, so knowing what the number is helps the firm's managers decide which projects to invest in. For potential investors, the firm's WACC tells you how much of a return the current investors are getting – and whether the firm might ultimately be worth more or less than that.

How to use it

Here is an example of a WACC calculation. Gryphon Conglomerate is a mid-sized firm assessing a few initiatives. To determine if any of these initiatives will deliver value to the firm, Gryphon is looking to calculate its WACC. Its shareholders, principally its founder and his family, started the company and continue to provide 80 per cent of its equity capital. They are looking for a 25 per cent rate of return on their money. The other 20 per cent consists of long-term debt, with an interest rate of 6 per cent.

Let's assume the marginal tax rate is 30 per cent. If it were 100 per cent equity-financed, its weighted average cost of capital would be 25 per cent. With debt, its WACC (using the formula shown above) is as follows:

$$
\begin{aligned}
\text{WACC} &= \frac{E}{V} \times R_e + \frac{D}{V} \times R_d \times (1 - T_c) \\
&= \frac{0.80}{1.00} \times 0.25 + \frac{0.20}{1.00} \times 0.06 \times (1 - 30\%) \\
&= 0.20 + 0.0084 \\
&= 0.2084, \text{ or } 20.84\%
\end{aligned}
$$

With this WACC in mind, each initiative has to have the potential to achieve an average annual return greater than 20.84 per cent for Gryphon to consider it. This is, in reality, a pretty high number. Even initiatives with a target return of 15–18 per cent per year would not be viable for Gryphon, although they would be for many other firms.

Since other firms in its industry use a greater proportion of debt in their capital structure (50 per cent on average), Gryphon decides to take on more debt, until it reaches the industry average. Its new WACC is shown here:

$$\text{WACC} = \frac{0.50}{1.00} \times 0.25 + \frac{0.50}{1.00} \times 0.06 \times (1 - 30\%)$$

$$= 0.125 + 0.021$$

$$= 0.146, \text{ or } 14.6\%$$

With its new capital structure, Gryphon can take on initiatives that have the potential to earn 15–18 per cent per annum because the potential returns are higher than its WACC.

What if Gryphon takes it one step further and attempts to finance itself with 80 per cent debt? Here is its revised, *hypothetical,* WACC:

$$\text{WACC} = \frac{0.20}{1.00} \times 0.25 + \frac{0.80}{1.00} \times 0.06 \times (1 - 30\%)$$

$$= 0.05 + 0.0336$$

$$= 0.0836, \text{ or } 8.36\%$$

One can see that as the proportion of debt (which carries a lower cost) increases, the WACC goes down. But this new WACC is hypothetical because as Gryphon takes on more debt, it takes on more risk for its equity holders, who will be worried about the company's ability to service the debt. The equity holders may, as a result of the increased risk of bankruptcy, demand a higher return on their investment. The impact of a higher cost of equity will then increase the WACC.

In calculating the WACC for a firm, investors generally want to know what the firm's target capital structure will look like, and this target is usually based on what is typical in the industry. For example, one might expect to see a higher proportion of debt used in real-estate investment trusts compared to firms in the high-tech sector.

How do you calculate the cost of debt and the cost of equity? The cost of debt is easy to estimate – you can simply look at the average interest paid on its existing long-term debt (or you can use the numbers from comparable firms). To calculate the cost of equity, one option is to use the 'capital asset pricing model' (CAPM), which provides an estimate based on the risk-free rate, the market return and how volatile the share price has been in the recent past. The second option is to use the dividend discount model, which provides an estimate based on dividend pay-outs. The third option is to estimate a risk premium on top of the current risk-free bond yield. For example, if the current 10-year US government bond is yielding 4 per cent and the market risk premium is 5 per cent, then the cost of equity for the firm would be 9 per cent.

Top practical tip

Estimating the WACC for a firm is a relatively straightforward calculation, because it is based on assumptions that make intuitive sense, and it does not involve difficult calculations. However, it is worth bearing in mind that, for many uses, a 'back-of-the-envelope' calculation is actually all that is required. For example, if you are trying to decide whether a significant capital investment is worth pursuing, you need to know roughly what the firm's WACC is (i.e. within 1–2 per cent), because the margin of error around the investment's returns is likely to be far greater than 1–2 per cent.

> ### Top pitfall
>
> Calculating the cost of equity requires estimates to be made. For example, if CAPM is used, one has to determine whether the current risk-free rate is an anomaly, whether the stock's past performance (in comparison to the market's performance) is likely to continue, and what the current market risk premium should be. Using different estimates will yield different results for the cost of equity.

Further reading

Allen, F.B. (1954) 'Does going into debt lower the "cost of capital"?' *The Analysts Journal*, 10(4): 57–61.

Miles, J.A. and Ezzell, J.R. (1980) 'The weighted average cost of capital, perfect capital markets, and project life: A clarification', *Journal of Financial and Quantitative Analysis*, 15(3): 719–730.

Modigliani, F. and Miller, M. (1958) 'The cost of capital, corporation finance and the theory of investment', *American Economic Review*, 48(3): 261–297.

Useful books to read next

There are vast numbers of books written on each of the topics we cover here. Here are a few useful ones to get you started, a mixture of texts as well as seminal contributions from luminaries in the field.

Management

Leading Change by John P. Kotter (Harvard Business Review Press, 2012)

Kotter is probably the leading authority on change management. This is his guide to how leaders achieve change.

Thinking Fast and Slow by Daniel Kahneman (Penguin, 2012)

This book is the definitive guide to behavioural psychology, from the Nobel Laureate who helped to create the field.

Organizational Behavior by Stephen Robbins and Timothy Judge (Pearson, 16th edition, 2014)

There are many good overview textbooks on organisational behaviour – this is one of the most well known and longest-established of them.

Managing by Henry Mintzberg (Financial Times/Prentice Hall, 2011)

Mintzberg has written many books on management in a 50-year career; this recent one summarises everything he has found.

Marketing and operations

Marketing Management by Philip T. Kotler and K.L. Keller (Pearson, 15th edition, 2015)

Kotler has been the top marketing guru for decades and this book is still the must-read text for students of marketing.

Influence: The psychology of persuasion by Robert Cialdini (HarperBusiness, 2007)

This book explains all the clever tricks marketers use to get people to buy their products.

The Long Tail by Chris Anderson (Hyperion Books, 2006)

Many recent books have examined how marketing changes as a result of the internet. This book was one of the first, and is still one of the best.

Positioning: The battle for your mind by Al Ries and Jack Trout (McGraw-Hill Education, 2001)

An all-time classic marketing book, it explains how segmentation and positioning work.

Strategy

Blue Ocean Strategy: How to create uncontested market space and make the competition irrelevant by W. Chan Kim & Renee Mauborgne (Harvard Business Review Press, 2015)

This book provides a definitive guide to how you define a distinctive and novel strategy.

Contemporary Strategy Analysis by Robert M. Grant (John Wiley & Sons, 2015)

A classic textbook, which does the best job of surveying the entire field of strategy.

Good Strategy Bad Strategy by Richard P. Rumelt (Profile Books Ltd, 2012)

An overview and critique of the various schools of strategy thinking, by one of the founders of the field.

Good to Great by Jim Collins (Random House Business, 2001)

This book is about strategy implementation – how to get your organisation mobilised around a distinctive purpose.

Innovation and entrepreneurship

Innovation and Entrepreneurship by John Bessant and Joe Tidd (John Wiley & Sons, 3rd edition, 2015)

A comprehensive text, looking at all the different aspects of innovation from a corporate and individual-entrepreneur perspective.

The Innovator's Dilemma by Clayton Christensen (Harvard Business Review Press, 2016)

The original book on 'disruptive' technologies, which made Christensen world famous.

The New Business Road Test by John Mullins (FT Press, 2013)

A very good overview textbook for anyone who wants to start a new business.

The Lean Startup by Eric Ries (Portfolio Penguin, 2011)

The hottest idea in the world of entrepreneurship today.

Finance

Investment Valuation: Tools and techniques for determining the value of any asset by Aswath Damodaran (John Wiley & Sons, 2012)

Written by *the* expert in the field, *Investment Valuation* goes over valuation techniques and, importantly, alerts readers to the various risks involved and how to mitigate them.

Principles of Corporate Finance by Richard A. Brealey, Stewart C. Myers and Franklin Allen (McGraw-Hill Education, 2016)

One of the standard texts on corporate finance and asset valuation, written with the financial manager in mind.

Horngren's Financial & Managerial Accounting, The Managerial Chapters by Tracie L. Miller-Nobles, Brenda L. Mattison and Ella Mae Matsumura (Pearson, 2015)

A good introduction to accounting and financial statement analysis.

Financial Markets and Institutions by Frederic S. Mishkin and Stanley Eakins (Pearson, 2015)

Aimed at improving the understanding of the world of finance outside the firm.

Glossary of terms

Asset-based valuation Valuing the firm based solely on its balance sheet, focusing on the fair-market value of total assets minus total liabilities.

BATNA Best alternative to a negotiated agreement, or your walk-away position in a negotiation.

Beta A measure of how volatile a stock's value has been, relative to the market as a whole; one of the indicators of how 'risky' a particular stock is.

Blue ocean An uncontested market space, distinct from a red ocean in which many other firms are competing.

Business strategy The choices a firm makes in how one business unit competes in a particular market.

Capabilities How a firm deploys its resources; 'distinctive' capabilities are those that the firm does better than others.

Capital asset pricing model (CAPM) Helps to estimate an expected return for a firm's equity holders.

Capital budgeting A technique to evaluate the potential profitability of various (and large) capital investments.

Channel The way a firm reaches its customers. For example, a bank will have a retail branch network, and also a telephone service and an internet- or mobile-based service; these are the bank's different channels to market.

Cognitive bias The not-entirely rational and sometimes inaccurate way someone looks at the world, perhaps because of prior experiences or the availability of information.

Comparable transaction valuation Valuing the firm by comparing it to its peer group.

Competitive advantage A position in a given market that gives a firm a superior return to that of its competitors.

Competitive position A chosen position in a given market – for example, low-cost, high-quality or focus.

Core competence A bundle of capabilities and resources that a firm can use across a number of different businesses or markets.

Corporate strategy The choices made by the firm about how it competes across multiple businesses, especially in terms of how it achieves synergies across them.

Cost of debt Expectation of returns from debt-holders willing to lend to the firm.

Cost of equity Expectation of returns from shareholders willing to invest in the firm.

Crowdsourcing Making use of large numbers of people to come up with or evaluate ideas; increasingly used in innovation processes in companies.

Culture The collective beliefs of people in an organisation; the unwritten rules about 'how we do things around here'.

Discount rate When referred to in valuation, the discount rate used is the weighted average cost of capital.

Discounted cash flow Computing a value for an asset or firm given a stream of future cash flows and a cost of capital.

Diversification A shift into adjacent markets, countries or business areas.

Dividend discount model   Valuing a firm by using the dividend stream it intends to return to investors.

Dynamic pricing   Rapid changes in the price you charge in response to demand.

Economies of scale   The reduction in costs of a product achieved by making it in large volumes.

Emergent strategy   The pattern of actions that takes shape over time, often not exactly the same as the intended strategy of the firm.

EQ or Emotional Intelligence   The ability to monitor your own and other people's emotions.

Five forces analysis   Invented by Michael Porter, this is a way of defining how profitable an industry is likely to be by looking at its overall structure – the internal rivalry, threat of new entrants, potential substitutes, supplier bargaining power and customer bargaining power.

Generic strategies   The three basic positions you can have in a market – low-cost, focus and differentiation – as defined by Michael Porter.

Groupthink   The notion that people working closely in a team end up sharing similar views and agreeing with each other too readily.

Innovator's dilemma   When faced with a disruptive technology (qv), established firms have to decide whether and when to adopt the new technology, with the risk that doing so means cannibalising existing sales.

Internal rate of return   The rate of return, as a percentage, that gives a project a net present value of zero.

Motivation   The underlying driver of individual effort in an organisational setting, often separated into intrinsic (from within) and extrinsic (from someone else).

Net present value The net value of all future cash flows associated with the project, discounted to the present day.

Open innovation   An umbrella term to describe how firms can make use of sources of insight and funding from people outside their boundaries in order to innovate more effectively.

Parenting advantage The ability of the corporate centre or 'parent' to add more value to a business unit than any other potential parent.

Performance appraisal The formalised way individuals receive feedback on how they are doing in an organisation.

Personalised marketing The notion that a product or service can be tailored to the specific needs of one individual.

Portfolio The set of businesses or markets that exists in a multi-business company.

Ratio analysis A methodology for analysing and making sense of a company's financial statements.

Resource-based view A way of looking at strategy that starts with an analysis of the firm's distinctive resources and capabilities.

Resources A firm's productive assets – for example, human, physical, financial or technological; they can be tangible or intangible in nature.

Risk-free rate The return an investor might expect from a risk-free investment; one example is a risk-free bond issued by a reliable government.

Scenario A coherent point of view about one possible way the future will transpire.

Segment A coherent subset of potential customers that might be targeted by a company.

Stage/gate process A formalised set of reviews that firms put in place to decide which innovation ideas to invest in and develop further.

Strategy The choices a firm makes about how and where it competes.

Vision A firm's 'vision statement' describes the 'intended future state' – for example, leadership in a particular industry. Sometimes the word 'purpose' is used instead of vision. 'Mission' is another close synonym, but it is usually used to mean a timeless *raison d'etre* for the firm – a statement of why it exists.

Weighted average cost of capital A financial metric used to measure the cost of capital to a firm. It is a weighted average of the firm's cost of debt and its cost of equity.

What did you think of this book?

We're really keen to hear from you about this book, so that we can make our publishing even better.

Please log on to the following website and leave us your feedback.

It will only take a few minutes and your thoughts are invaluable to us.

www.pearsoned.co.uk/bookfeedback

Index

Page numbers in **bold** refer to glossary definitions.